JourneyThrough®
Mark

62 Devotional Insights by **Robert M. Solomon**

Journey Through Mark
© 2016 by Robert M. Solomon
All rights reserved.

Discovery House is affiliated
with Our Daily Bread Ministries.

Requests for permission to quote
from this book should be directed to:
Permissions Department
Discovery House
P.O. Box 3566
Grand Rapids, MI 49501
Or contact us by email at
permissionsdept@dhp.org

Design by Joshua Tan
Typeset by Grace Goh

ISBN 978-1-62707-820-7

Printed in the USA
First Printing in 2017

Foreword

In the New Testament epistles, we read doctrinal truths about God and their implications for Christian living. Several of these were written before any of the four gospels. In the decades following the death and resurrection of Jesus, there was a growing need for Christians to read about what He actually said and did. Thus the Gospels came to be written. They provide four portraits of Jesus that together help us to meet Him in person. Mark's gospel is believed to be the earliest of these portraits.

In reading Mark, we encounter the living Christ—who He is, what He said, and what He did, especially on the cross. It is important to read this gospel carefully, slowly, with reverence and anticipation. Such reading will bring to life the vivid scenes painted by the gospel writer, just as if you are actually present. You will find yourself hearing the words of Jesus, witnessing His miraculous deeds, or observing the reactions of those around Him. You may also hear the Lord speaking to you personally as you read and meditate upon the Word. If so, it is important that you learn to respond to Him from your heart, for in so doing, your life will be changed by His grace.

Jesus invites you to meet Him, more deeply than you have done before. It is an invitation to a personal encounter and conversation as you follow Him through all the wonderful scenes painted in the gospel. Like many who met Him 2,000 years ago, as recorded by Mark, you will be amazed as you discover who He is and what He has done for you. He will inspire you to follow Him, for He is our Servant King, who died for us and lives forevermore.

To God be the glory,
Robert M. Solomon

We're glad you've decided to join us on a journey into a deeper relationship with Jesus Christ!

For over 50 years, we have been known for our daily Bible reading notes, *Our Daily Bread*. Many readers enjoy the pithy, inspiring, and relevant articles that point them to God and the wisdom and promises of His unchanging Word.

Building on the foundation of *Our Daily Bread*, we have developed this devotional series to help believers spend time with God in His Word, book by book. We trust this daily meditation on God's Word will draw you into a closer relationship with Him through our Lord and Savior, Jesus Christ.

How to use this resource

READ: This book is designed to be read alongside God's Word as you journey with Him. It offers explanatory notes to help you understand the Scriptures in fresh ways.

REFLECT: The questions are designed to help you respond to God and His Word, letting Him change you from the inside out.

RECORD: The space provided allows you to keep a diary of your journey as you record your thoughts and jot down your responses.

An Overview

The shortest of the four gospels, and probably the earliest, Mark brings us to Jesus Christ (Christ means Messiah, or the Anointed One) without much fanfare and lengthy introduction. Tradition has it that Mark got much of his material from the apostle Peter, with whom he was closely associated (1 Peter 5:13). This is supported by scholarly examinations of the gospel itself. It portrays Jesus as a man of action and focuses on His deeds more than His words. In the words of New Testament scholar A. T. Robertson, it "throbs with life and bristles with vivid details."[1]

The gospel can be divided into two major sections, with Peter's confession that Jesus is the Messiah in Mark 8:27–30 serving as a hinge. The first part introduces Jesus as the Son of God, the Messiah, and more importantly, the Servant King. It shows what it takes to be God's obedient servant, by tracing the work of Jesus as it develops among needy humanity. In the process, His compassion, authority, power, and sense of mission are demonstrated.

However, the story shifts to a darker mood after Peter's confession, describing the Servant King's suffering and eventual death on the cross at the hands of His enemies. The heavy price Jesus paid for complete obedience to His Father's will lets readers understand that their devotion to the Servant King may likewise lead them to face persecution and even death. But Jesus's powerful resurrection dispels all gloom, enabling His faithful followers to face suffering with purpose and hope.

Overall, Mark's gospel challenges readers to respond to its message: trust in the Servant King, believe He is the Son of God who is the Messiah, and faithfully follow Him all the way.

Mark can be divided as follows:

1:1–13   An Introduction to the Son of God
1:14–8:30 The Servant King at Work
8:31–15:47 The Servant King Opposed and Killed
16:1–20   The Servant King's Resurrection and the Good News to the World

---

[1] A. T. Robertson, *Word Pictures of the New Testament Volume One: The Gospel According to Matthew and the Gospel According to Mark*, rev. and updated by Wesley J. Perschbacher (Grand Rapids: Kregel Publications, 2004), 259.

Day 1

Read Mark 1:1–8

The birthday of the Roman emperor Augustus Caesar was celebrated throughout the Empire as "good news" and, with much pomp and grandiosity, he was declared the "Son of God." These two phrases were common knowledge among Roman subjects, and Mark begins his gospel by linking these phrases to the Old Testament and to Jesus Christ instead (v. 1). This radical message challenged the claims of the imperial authorities in Rome: who were they compared to the King of kings? Caesar's claim to special authority was challenged by the absolute authority of Christ, just as all mortal rulers are, for Jesus is the same yesterday, today, and forever (Hebrews 13:8). **The rest of the gospel introduces the reader to this Christ, who is divine and is good news to the world.**

Mark quotes Malachi 3:1 and Isaiah 40:3 in announcing that the Lord and Messiah had come. His coming had been prophesied in the Old Testament, and now, after about 400 years of divine silence, the special messenger foretold in the last book of the Old Testament had finally come to prepare the way for the Lord. This messenger was John the Baptist, who ministered in the wilderness by "preaching a baptism of repentance" (v. 4). John was a rugged individual who dressed like the Old Testament prophet Elijah (2 Kings 1:8). Jesus later said in Mark 9:12–13 that John came like Elijah, confirming the fulfillment of the prophecy in Malachi 4:5 (cf. Matthew 11:14; Isaiah 40:3). John prepared the people for the coming of the Lord by urging them to confess their sins and be baptized in the Jordan River.

John's baptism was reminiscent of the Israelites' exodus experience: coming out of Egypt through the Red Sea. It challenged the people to repent—to come out of sin—and undergo a second exodus through the waters of baptism in preparation for a new covenant with God (Isaiah 51:10–11).

John described the coming Messiah as one far more important than he (Mark 1:7–8). Jesus was more powerful and far greater, and John felt unworthy to even untie His sandals. Jesus also provided a baptism far superior to John's. While John only baptized with water (to symbolize repentance that precedes such baptism), Jesus will baptize with the Holy Spirit (to bring transformation into holiness that follows such a spiritual baptism).

There is something unique about this Jesus, an individual completely unprecedented in human history. Good news indeed!

Think of all the "good news" the powers-that-be and marketplaces of the world offer. Why do they pale in the light of the good news of Jesus Christ? Why is it and how has it been good news to you personally?

What does repentance mean and what does it involve? Reflect on the message of repentance and the two kinds of baptism (v. 8). What is the relationship between repentance and spiritual transformation?

Day 2

Read Mark 1:9–13

Verse 9 simply states that Jesus was baptized by John. But if John's baptism signified repentance, why did Jesus ask for it? Matthew 3:14–15 gives us a fuller picture of events. John in fact recoiled from the idea of baptizing Jesus because he knew Jesus was sinless. It was John who needed to be baptized by Jesus! John consented only because Jesus said that it was necessary to "fulfill all righteousness" (Matthew 3:15). Jesus was baptized not for any sin of His but for our sins. He came to identify with us so that He could carry our sins to the cross and die for us.

Something remarkable happened when Jesus was baptized. Heaven was torn open and the Holy Spirit descended on Jesus (v. 10). The Father's voice declared to Jesus, "You are my Son, whom I love; with you I am well pleased" (v. 11). This echoed Psalm 2:7 ("You are my son") and Isaiah 42:1 ("Here is my servant . . . in whom I delight") and reiterated the identity of Jesus: He is the Son and Servant of God. This baptism is a prototype for all Christian baptisms, for **our baptism reminds us of our identity in Christ**. We are God's children and servants, initiated into God's family and commissioned into His service.

Note how the three persons in the Trinity were united at the Jordan River (Mark 1:10–11). Salvation is the work of the Father, Son, and Holy Spirit, who unite perfectly to save us from sin and death. What a wonderful, comforting, and reassuring truth!

The Greek word for "at once" (*euthus*) in verse 12 is a frequent occurrence (it is used more than 40 times, translated variously as "immediately," "at once," "without delay," "quickly," and "just then") in Mark's fast-moving gospel. The Spirit "sent him out" (the Greek word is very strong, best translated as "drove" or "expelled") into the desert (v. 12). Jesus spent 40 days there and was tempted by Satan. Further details are provided by Matthew (4:1–11) and Luke (4:1–13). Jesus fasted as He dealt with Satan's temptations. He also faced danger from wild animals, but was assisted by angels, who strengthened Him.

Between Jesus's baptism and service, between His calling and ministry, lies temptation. This is a lesson that applies to all who commit their lives to following Christ and obeying His call to service. We can see from Matthew 4:3–9 that Satan was a master at twisting God's words and sowing doubt. Knowing that Jesus had just received the approval of the Father, Satan challenged Him to prove His divinity, taunting, "If you are the Son of God . . ." (4:3, 6). He then proposed short cuts and diversions from the cross (4:8–9).

How does Jesus identify with us in both His baptism and temptation (Hebrews 2:14; 4:15)? According to Matthew 3:13–15 and Romans 6:1–10, why was Jesus baptized and what does it say about your own baptism? If your baptism helps you to be united with Jesus, what are the implications for the way you live?

How can we safeguard ourselves against the temptations of Satan that are found between calling and ministry? What is your own experience in this regard?

Day 3

Read Mark 1:14–20

Baptized into His mission and victorious over temptation, Jesus began His public ministry. He came into prominence as John, having been arrested, receded into the shadows (v. 14).

Jesus started preaching the good news, which was from Him and about Him. His opening words indicated several truths. His appearing was timely (the Greek word indicates an opportune and right time). The kingdom of God had come near (v. 15), it was not far away or just a philosophical idea. It was near because God, in Christ, had come near. There is a two-fold response God expects of us: repentance and belief. To repent is to change direction (away from sin and toward God), without which one cannot enter the kingdom. To believe is to entrust one's life to God; more than intellectual knowledge, it is a relationship that is centered on personal trust. **Jesus ushered in His kingdom, which one enters by repenting of one's sins and in which one remains by continuing to trust Him (v. 15). He is the good news.**

Jesus then chose four disciples (two sets of brothers). They were simple fishermen; God often chooses what in the eyes of the world is foolish, weak, and lowly (1 Corinthians 1:27–29)—He will accomplish His purposes through His own grace and power. He graciously invites us to participate in His mission. "Come, follow me" (Mark 1:17) is the primary task of the disciple. Put away all other things of value and return to this simplest and deepest call to follow Jesus. We must keep returning to Him as we are easily distracted and drift away. We must keep following Him—not the crowd, nor our own heart.

To follow Jesus is to let Him lead us and being willing to leave everything to do so. Nothing is so precious or important that it cannot be left behind to follow Jesus. "At once" the disciples "left their nets and followed him" (v. 18). Two of them even "left their father" (v. 20).

"I will make you . . ." (v. 17, ESV). It is Jesus who makes us fishers of men, or anything else He wants us to be. He enables us and it is often an ongoing process. We must remember that all our competence comes from God (2 Corinthians 3:4–6).

Reflect on Christ's call to repent and believe. How have you experienced this? Is the Lord speaking to you today about repenting and believing?

Jesus called fishermen to be fishers of men, just as he called Moses, who was working as a shepherd, to shepherd His people out of Egypt. Nothing is wasted in God's economy. In what way do you see your past training and experiences being relevant to your present ministry for the Lord?

Day 4

Read Mark 1:21–39

Imagine a pastor who has had an extremely busy and exhausting Sunday. He returns home to take a well-earned rest. Then there's a knock on the door, and his whole church is outside. The same thing happened to Jesus. After a busy Sabbath day ministering to the people in Capernaum, Jesus went to Peter's home to rest. There He graciously healed Peter's mother-in-law (vv. 29–31). That evening, "the whole town gathered at the door" asking for Jesus's help. He had compassion on the crowd and "healed many" and "drove out many demons" (vv. 33–34).

The ministry of Jesus was characterized by His compassion (see Mark 1:41; 6:34) and authority. Earlier in the day, Jesus taught in the synagogue; His listeners were "amazed at his teaching" because "he taught them as one who had authority" (v. 22). People recognized authority residing in Him. He showed the same authority when He casts out an evil spirit from a demonized man (vv. 23–27) and healed people (vv. 33–34).

The third characteristic of the ministry of Jesus was His faithfulness. We are not sure if Jesus got any sleep that night, having to minister to such a large number of troubled and needy people. But no matter how little sleep He had, He still did not take a much-deserved day off. Instead, He woke up really early to spend time with His Father. Mark, who is usually economical with his words, emphasizes this point: "Very early in the morning, while it was still dark . . ." (v. 35). **Jesus showed us that no amount of busyness should deter us from spending time with God, without which our ministry will run dry or run aground.**

It is because Jesus spent time with His Father in prayer that He was able to see through the subtle temptation presented by the disciples, who were frantically searching for Him. "Everyone is looking for you!" they exclaimed (v. 37). It was nice to be needed and tempting to remain in Capernaum. Instead, Jesus told His disciples, "Let us go somewhere else—to the nearby villages" (v. 38). Other places needed to hear Him. There was work to be done. "That is why I have come"—Jesus was faithful to the calling and mission that His Father gave Him.

ThinkThrough

Consider the three characteristics of the ministry of Jesus. What do they say about who Jesus is? Prayerfully examine how each of these characteristics find expression in the way the Lord relates and ministers to you.

The disciples bring news of how popular Jesus has become in Capernaum, but no matter how tempting it is to remain, Jesus continues on with His mission. What can you learn from Jesus that is applicable to your own experience?

Day 5

Read Mark 1:40–2:12

Jesus was like a brilliant bolt of lightning that illuminates the night sky, except that He was not just a momentary flash, but a brilliant beacon of light. Such were His amazing acts, that it is understandable why people remarked with great wonder, "We have never seen anything like this!" (Mark 2:12).

A man with leprosy (a most terrible disease in the ancient world) humbly approached Jesus on his knees for help. He showed great faith when he said: "If you are willing, you can make me clean" (Mark 1:40). Jesus replied that He was willing and commanded, "Be clean!" (1:41).

The man did not doubt Jesus's ability to heal, but was unsure if He was willing to do so. Jesus had both power and love, for He was "moved with pity" (Mark 1:41, ESV) and touched the man, something no other person would do for fear of becoming infected.

Jesus warned him not to tell others about the miracle, but the man could not keep such news to himself. As a result, Jesus became so popular that He could "no longer enter a town openly" (1:45). Throughout his writing, Mark consistently shows that Jesus did not want fame as a healer to become a hindrance to His ministry of teaching (cf. 2:2).

Jesus returned to Capernaum and healed a paralyzed man (Mark 2:1–12), who somehow must have missed the great healings that had taken place there recently (1:32–34). Unable to walk, he was carried in by some concerned men (friends, relatives, or neighbors). This time the poor man found the crowd to be an added obstacle, but his plucky friends opened up the roof and let him down in front of Jesus, who saw their faith and healed the man (2:5). Unlike the leper, faith was found in those who carried the sick man.

Initially Jesus told the paralyzed man, "Son, your sins are forgiven" (Mark 2:5) which made the teachers of the law condemn Jesus in their hearts as a blasphemer—for only God had that authority (2:6–7). Jesus asked them which would be easier: to heal the man or to declare his sins forgiven (2:9). They knew that the act would be more difficult than the words. Jesus then declared that He had authority to forgive sins (an invisible reality) and proved it with a visibly powerful healing (2:10–12).

Does one need to have faith to be healed? Which is actually easier—to declare forgiveness or to heal? What do these stories of healing tell you about Jesus?

Reflect on what Jesus is doing in your life. Are you astounded? Are you telling others about it? Is there a friend you need to bring to Jesus?

Day 6

Read Mark 2:13–17

When Jesus passes by, expect your life to change significantly. This is what happened to a tax collector working in Capernaum, beside the Sea of Galilee. His name was Levi (also known as Matthew; see Matthew 9:9). He was a tax collector, an occupation coveted by those who desired a quick path to riches and hated by those who suffered under heavy Roman taxes. Tax collectors were authorized to gather money on behalf of Rome from the local population based on an official rate per head or unit of weight of cargo, but could overcharge and keep the excess for themselves. They were thus widely hated as traitors and cheats.

Capernaum was an important port on the Sea of Galilee. Large quantities of goods passed through and were conveniently taxed. Levi was busy with his lucrative business when Jesus spotted him. He must have viewed him with compassion and with the knowledge of one who looks into the hearts of people. He said only two words, "Follow me," (v. 14) and Levi immediately left his job and followed Jesus. Perhaps his heart had been in turmoil lately, or something in the face and voice of Jesus convinced him, but Levi left a profitable business to follow Jesus.

He invited Jesus to his house for a meal. It may have been a farewell party for his fellow tax-collectors, but what a witness Levi turned out to be! It appeared that he wanted his friends to meet Jesus as well. Converted people often opened their homes in gratitude and generosity (cf. Acts 10:48; 16:15, 34). The fault-finding Pharisees criticized Jesus for mixing with sinful tax collectors. Jesus answered that it was normal for a physician to be with sick patients, and He was the physician of the soul (v. 17). It was sad that the Pharisees, who were the really soul-sick ones, recognized neither their need nor Jesus as the soul physician who could heal them.

As long as people deny their spiritual condition, they will remain unhealed. The tax collectors and sinners in Capernaum who believed in Jesus were blessed when they met and followed Him.

ThinkThrough

Note that the passage begins with Jesus teaching a large crowd (v. 13). He did what He came to do. How important are the teachings of Jesus? How important are they to you?

The call of Jesus is simple yet profound: "Follow me" (Mark 1:17; 2:14). Imagine Jesus coming to your regular place of work—at home, in church, or in your workplace. What do His words mean to you personally and how are you following Jesus? Is there anything you need to leave in order to follow Jesus?

Day 7

Read Mark 2:18–3:6

As His popularity rose, Jesus began to encounter opposition. This passage opens with questions meant to discredit Jesus and ends with a plot to kill Him.

The Pharisees claimed to uphold the Law of Moses, but were in fact defending the heavy scaffolding—the additional rules and regulations—they had built up around the Law. In so doing they had distorted the Law and led people away from its real requirements. Two examples are given here: fasting (Mark 2:18–22) and the Sabbath (2:23–3:6).

The Law required fasting on the annual Day of Atonement (Leviticus 16:29). Later, people fasted in times of national crisis, and on regular days for personal devotion. The Pharisees fasted twice a week (Luke 18:12) and made it into a strict rule and ritual and a way of impressing others (Matthew 6:16–18). When they noticed that Jesus's disciples did not fast like they did, they questioned Him (Mark 2:18). He reminded them that during weeklong wedding celebrations, fasting requirements were suspended because it was a time of joy. Jesus then declared Himself to be the heavenly Bridegroom. As long as He was around, it was a time of joy. Later, His disciples would fast when He was taken away (2:19–20). The relentless fault-finding continued. The hungry disciples were now faulted for helping themselves to the crops in the fields (Mark 2:23–24). This itself was allowed by the Law (Deuteronomy 23:25) but the Pharisees complained that they had broken the Sabbath. Presumably it had to do with reaping, threshing, or winnowing, all prohibited actions on Sabbath, but Mark doesn't specify. Nevertheless, Jesus replied that human need is more important than religious rituals (by using an incident in the life of David from 1 Samuel 21:1–6) and that He was the Lord of the Sabbath and had no problem with the actions of His disciples (Mark 2:25–27).

These points are further reiterated when Jesus healed a man with a shriveled hand (Mark 3:1–6). What began as indirect attacks (complaints about Jesus's disciples) now became a direct attack. Jesus felt deep emotion (anger and distress) over the "stubborn hearts" of His opponents. It was easier to heal shriveled hands than stubborn hearts. The Pharisees failed to realize that Jesus came to fulfill the true intent of the Law and thus usher in a new reality. His new wine could not be put into the old wineskins of Pharisaic tradition. **Stale rituals must be replaced with a new relationship with the living God.**

The Pharisees tried to follow their own rules rather than the divine Lawmaker. Think of times when you tend to do the same. How can you avoid it?

Religious legalists that practiced a strict form of Judaism, the Pharisees hated the Herodians for their political support of pagan Rome. But against Jesus, even such bitter enemies became allies (Mark 3:6). Do you see such collusions in society today? How should you then pray?

Day 8

Read Mark 3:7–19

Crowds from near and far followed Jesus (v. 8). They pushed Him to the edge of the Sea of Galilee and Jesus had to ask the disciples to prepare a small boat for Him to avoid being overwhelmed (v. 9). It seems that He preferred to teach them from the quiet and dignified distance of a boat in the water. But the crowd was more interested in His miracles; they had come because "they heard all he was doing" (v. 8). The crowd surged forward, eager to receive healing and satisfy their curiosity. Jesus had become a celebrity. There were also many demons acknowledging Jesus as the Son of God (v. 11). Just imagine the din from the combined human and demonic crowd.

The opposition against Jesus was gathering—the Pharisees and Herodians were plotting to kill Him. The frenzied crowds only wanted quick solutions and were not interested in listening to His message—they were more interested in what Jesus was doing than in who He claimed to be.

Jesus "went up on a mountainside" (v. 13), and Luke tells us that He prayed there the whole night (Luke 6:12). After praying, Jesus selected His disciples.

Twelve of them are named. They were to be apprenticed to Jesus.

This means two things. First, they were called to be with Jesus—to spend time with Him and learn from Him. Second, they were to be sent out by Jesus as His apostles (literally the sent ones, v. 14). They were to primarily preach (v. 14), and if they encountered demonic opposition, they were given authority to drive it out (v. 15).

Perhaps in view of the plots to kill Him and the growing crowds, it had become necessary for Jesus to form this group. But more importantly, after His death and resurrection, these men (though full of weaknesses) would continue the mission of Jesus. This took place subsequently when they received the Holy Spirit and became bold witnesses and martyrs for Christ. Jesus, while ministering to the crowds with compassion, ensured that He spent sufficient time with this group of disciples to prepare them for their critical task.

Would you agree that Jesus was more interested in teaching the crowds? Why do you think so? What are the implications for how the church carries out its ministry?

Jesus calls us to be apprenticed to Him. Reflect on the need to be with Him and to be sent out by Him. Assess your present life in terms of these two aspects of apprenticeship.

Read Mark 3:20–30

The crowds continued to grow. While Jesus was indoors, a crowd prevented Him and His disciples from having a meal (v. 20). Imagine a doctor in a clinic with hundreds of patients queuing up to see him. It is such a long queue that he has to skip lunch in order to attend to all of them. Jesus was in a similar situation. Two groups of people were assessing His actions: His family and a group of teachers of the law.

Jesus's family members were concerned about Him. He was endangering Himself by making the religious authorities angry with Him. Perhaps popularity was going to His head! His forgoing meals to minister to the crowds was the last straw— perhaps He was better off returning to His small, quiet business in Nazareth. They concluded that "He is out of his mind" and went to "take charge of him" (v. 21). It must have grieved Jesus to be misunderstood by those close to Him.

But more hurting was the condemnation from the teachers of the law, who had been sent by the authorities in Jerusalem to evaluate Jesus and His miracles. Their conclusion: "He is possessed by Beelzebul!" otherwise known as the "prince of demons" (v. 22). They accused Jesus of being possessed by Satan himself—that must have been why He could perform so many miracles.

Jesus countered them by asking "How can Satan drive out Satan?" (v. 23). A divided house would not be able to stand. There was no civil war in the demonic kingdom; the real war was between the kingdom of God and Satan's hordes. Jesus declared Himself to be stronger than Satan— He had in fact been plundering Satan's dark kingdom by plucking individuals from his evil grasp (v. 27).

The learned but unwise scribes were in danger of committing the unpardonable sin, which is a sin of blasphemy against the Holy Spirit. To attribute the work of the Holy Spirit (John 15:26; 16:8) to Satan is the unpardonable sin. **In essence, if one continues to reject what the Holy Spirit does, he is guilty of the "eternal sin" from which he cannot be saved (v. 29), for he would not have repented and turned to Christ.**

ThinkThrough

Jesus was "diagnosed" to be mad and bad. How do you think He must have felt? Think of those times you have been misunderstood or maligned for doing God's work? What do you think Jesus would say to you?

How is Jesus "plundering" Satan's diabolical kingdom today? Where do you see yourself in what He is doing? Why is prayer vital?

Day 10

Read Mark 3:31–35

The family members of Jesus who wanted to "take charge of him" (v. 21) finally arrived on the scene. The house was crowded, so they stood outside and send word that they were waiting. His listeners expected Jesus to pause and answer the summons. After all, one was expected to treat one's mother and brothers with special affection and attention. But Jesus did not seem to be moved, nor did He move. Instead, He asked a puzzling question, "Who are my mother and my brothers?" (v. 33).

Why did Jesus respond to His family's presence in this seemingly cold and aloof way? That Jesus loved His mother Mary was clearly expressed by how He obeyed her in childhood (Luke 2:51) and provided for her when He was dying on the cross (John 19:26–27). Mary was probably there as any mother would be, worried for the well-being of her son (even though He was now an adult). But Jesus's brothers had responded differently to Him; they did not believe His claims and message (John 7:5). Only after His resurrection would they be convinced of who He really was (Acts 1:14). Instead, they had come to make Him see reason

and return home with them. In either case, the appearance of the family was an intrusion and interruption.

Jesus then looked at those around Him and said, "Whoever does God's will is my brother and sister and mother" (v. 35). **He was redefining His family as comprising those who would do God's will.**

When He came down to earth, He said, "I have come to do your will" (Hebrews 10:7) and in His ministry He made it clear that, "My food is to do the will of him who sent me and to finish his work" (John 4:34). Those who believe in Him and follow Him must do likewise. In this they will resemble the Son of God and have the family semblance of the children of God. It is for this reason that those who will enter the kingdom of heaven will be those who had done the will of God (Matthew 7:21).

The scribes who had come to assess Jesus were likely present as well. Jesus extended His invitation to them. He does the same to us today.

Reflect on how Jesus carried out His Father's will in the face of temptations and distractions. What can we learn from His experience? How strong was His resolve to do nothing but His Father's will (John 5:17, 19, 30; 6:38; 8:28–29, 50)?

In what way is doing God's will a personal choice (John 7:17) and a divine enablement (Philippians 2:13)? What do you think is God's will for your life? How are you fulfilling His will in your life?

Day 11

Read Mark 4:1–20

Why is it that the reading and preaching of God's Word produces such a variety of responses in the congregation, from boredom to great excitement? Often, a congregation assesses the preacher and lays any blame at his feet. But in this parable, the preacher assessed the congregation. This well-known parable of the sower may be better titled "The Four Soils" because it is really about four kinds of responses to the Word of God.

Jesus made it clear that the seed represents the Word of God (v. 14). The farmer is the preacher (Jesus in this case). The four soils represent four kinds of people.

Some people are like the path; the seed that falls on it is taken away quickly by Satan (vv. 4, 15). Such people hear but fail to listen. They do not reflect on what is said or read, and, as they say, the message goes in one ear and comes out the other. Whenever the Word is sown, Satan will attempt to distract and divert people. A distracted, preoccupied, or skeptical person will not readily receive God's Word.

Some people are like the rocky soil (vv. 5, 16–17). There is an initial response to the Word, but it does not take root due to shallowness of heart. Charles Spurgeon once remarked that some people seem to have been baptized in "boiling water," requiring constant, superficial excitement to remain in the faith.[2] When trouble or persecution comes, such people will leave quickly. Their idea of discipleship has no place for suffering. They are fair-weather Christians.

Others are like the thorny ground (vv. 7, 18–19). They respond to the gospel but are overcome by worries, greed, and worldly desires that choke their spiritual life and prevent them from bearing spiritual fruit. They are not willing to give up the world to gain Christ.

It is the good soil that represents true disciples (vv. 8, 20). They accept God's Word and produce a rich harvest. Unlike the others, they are willing to really listen, to suffer, and to give up everything for Christ (Luke 14:33).

[2] C. H. Spurgeon, "No Root in Themselves" (sermon, Metropolitan Tabernacle, Newington, 23 September 1888).

Why do we need to let God's Word take root in our lives? How do we let it happen?

Assess your own discipleship in light of the four soils. How do you hear God's Word (Mark 4:9, 23–24)? Do you find all the different soils in your heart, in that your response to God's Word varies based on different areas of your life?

Day 12

Read Mark 4:21–25

The parable of the sower is followed later on by two other parables about seeds. In between are these four pithy sayings of Jesus that seem out of place among the parables. However, the connection can be seen in verses 23–24: "If anyone has ears to hear, let them hear. Consider carefully what you hear." These sayings have to do with the hearing and reception of God's Word, a matter introduced by the previous parable on the four kinds of response and their consequences.

The first saying indicates the responsibility of the one who hears the Word (v. 21). If he understands it, then it will enter his life as a light that is not to be kept to oneself but shared with others. In other words, the one into whose heart the seed of God's Word is sown must himself become a sower. There are evangelistic responsibilities for the disciple who hears and obeys. Becoming a sower is one of the fruits of a heart that is like the good soil. In His Sermon on the Mount, Jesus said something similar, reminding His listeners that they would be "the light of the world" if they let the light "shine before others" (Matthew 5:14–16).

The second saying (Mark 4:22) reiterates the first—the gospel light cannot be hidden away. But it could also refer to the fact that when God's Word comes into a person, it tests what is hidden, concealed from others or even from oneself. God's Word is like a torch that shines in the darkness. It exposes our sins, weaknesses, and self-serving excuses (Hebrews 4:12–13).

The third saying (Mark 4:24) indicates that God will reward our response to His Word. When we receive the Word with joy, faith, and obedience, we will be given more and a growing capacity for more. It takes time to grow in God's Word. God is always generous, "and even more," in His actions and responses to us. As His Word grows in us, His blessings too will grow.

The fourth saying (v. 25) repeated the third and also stated the obverse. **One who does not allow the Word to sink deeply into his life will be all the poorer for it. The adage "use it or lose it" comes to mind.**

How can you make it a habit to humbly share with others what the Lord has taught you? Is there someone with whom you should regularly share your insights?

What do the third and fourth sayings (vv. 24–25) say about discipleship as an ongoing process of faith, obedience, and understanding? How have you fared in this journey?

Day 13

Read Mark 4:26–34

Jesus introduced the next two parables by saying "This is what the kingdom of God is like" (vv. 26, 30). They are designed to deepen our understanding of the nature of the kingdom and how it works. The kingdom is the realm where Jesus is king—in our hearts, in the church, in society.

Taking its cue from the parable of the sower, we are again presented with the scene of a man sowing seed (v. 26). The miracle is that the seed grows into a plant and bears fruit. It grows all day and night, even when the sower sleeps (v. 27). How this happens cannot be explained other than that the divine power connected to God's Word is at work. God's Word will accomplish His purposes, and sowing it is not a wasted activity (Isaiah 55:10–11). The phrase "all by itself" (Mark 4:28) indicates the inherent power of God's Word and kingdom. When we obey God by sharing His Word with others, God's power is invisibly and secretly at work to demonstrate that it is God who truly causes the growth (1 Corinthians 3:6–7). The glory belongs to God alone.

The second parable (Mark 4:30–32) also paints a vivid picture of how God's power works in His kingdom. The farmer's smallest seed, the mustard seed, grows into the largest of garden plants (vv. 31–32). It has branches big enough for birds to perch on and provides helpful shade (v. 32). Again, we are led to understand the mystery and divine power connected with God's Word and how it works in His kingdom, especially in our hearts. We are reminded of the historical spread of the gospel across the globe; today Christianity is the largest religion in the world. The preaching of God's Word often resulted in the transformation of societies, nations, and civilizations. **The Word has not lost any of its power today. We should continue to read it, mediate on it, obey it, and spread it by preaching, teaching, and sharing.**

ThinkThrough

Jesus spoke in parables (vv. 33–34). Why do you think He did this? Why did He have to explain His parables to His disciples in private? Has your understanding of the parables of Jesus grown deeper over time?

If God is the one who gives growth, what does that say about our attitude when we share God's Word or help disciple someone? Why is prayer so important in this process?

Day 14

Read Mark 4:35–41

The Sea of Galilee was a lake surrounded by hills. Sudden storms were not uncommon. Jesus and His disciples were crossing by boat in the evening when a "furious squall" (v. 37) suddenly sprung up and created big, threatening waves, all the more terrifying in the darkness. The boat was "nearly swamped." This was a storm so big, even the seasoned fishermen were afraid.

Jesus was on the boat too, but tired from a busy day of preaching, He was sleeping at the back, oblivious to the disciples' desperate attempts to keep the boat afloat. They woke Him up and, with a hint of reproach, asked, "Teacher, don't you care if we drown" (v. 38). What a question! When we are afraid or angry, we are all too ready to blame others.

Jesus got up and taught them a lesson about His amazing power. He rebuked the wind and commands the waves to be still, and they obeyed (v. 39). The disciples were stunned to see such tremendous power and authority. Besides showing that even nature obeyed Him, Jesus also gave His disciples an impromptu lesson concerning His presence. If He was present, then no matter how terrible the storm, the disciples should have trusted that they would be safe. But instead they fearfully appealed to Jesus to do something about the storm. To them, His presence alone was not enough, but between His presence and power, the more desirable was the former, for it included the latter as well. The frightened disciples needed to learn this lesson and put their confidence in Jesus.

There was a deeper lesson still. If the disciples recalled that Jesus had earlier declared, "Let us go over to the other side" (v. 35), they would have understood that His purpose was unchanging and inevitable—if He intended to reach his destination, they would arrive safely. **The same applied to His promises: if He said so, it would happen.**

Later the disciples saw Jesus arrested and tortured. His power seemed to be absent as He suffered cruel crucifixion. His presence was also absent the following day. But if they had remembered this lesson from the perfect storm, they would have been comforted by His purpose and promise: that He would rise from the dead (Mark 10:33–34), just as He said. What a precious lesson!

ThinkThrough

What has been your understanding and experience of the power, presence, and purposes of Christ? In which of these do you need to grow, especially when you are going through difficult times?

Jesus asked the disciples, "Why are you so afraid? Do you still have no faith?" (v. 40). Has He ever spoken to you this way? What is the faith He is talking about? Faith in what or whom?

Day 15

Read Mark 5:1–20

A demon-possessed person can be a frightening sight. Jesus and His disciples met such a man in the Gerasenes, an area largely occupied by Gentiles. The poor man was in a terrible state, homeless and living in the cemeteries. He was also naked and shameless (Luke 8:27). Having lost his sanity and self-control, he cut himself with stones. Even chains could not hold him still. "No one was strong enough to subdue him" (v. 4). Possessed by a legion of demons for a long time (v. 9), the man was a miserable wreck. He had become a resident of hell even on earth.

Jesus commanded the demon to come out of the man (v. 8). The man rushed to Jesus (imagine the fear of the disciples) but fell on his knees. A loud demonic voice spoke, asking Jesus not to torture them (v. 7). This was ironic as the demons were the ones tormenting the man. Jesus asked for the demon's name, and it replied that it was Legion (suggesting that there are many of them). The demon begged Jesus not to expel them from the region. Mark does not record why they wanted to stay in the region, but Jesus granted their request to enter a herd of pigs nearby. The pigs rushed with demonic frenzy down a steep slope and drowned in the lake (vv. 11–13). This dramatic exorcism was probably to reassure the man that he had been healed and delivered.

Unlike in his possessed state, the man was now resting (sitting), dressed, and had regained his sanity (v. 15). What an amazing change! But instead of being happy, the people in the area were "afraid" (v. 15). We wonder why. Were they worried about losing more pigs, or that more demons would be exposed among them? Amazingly, they pleaded with Jesus to leave their region instead of gladly welcoming Him (v. 17).

This passage portrays the demons begging Jesus not to expel them from the region (v. 10), the people begging Jesus to leave the very same region (v. 17), and the healed man begging to be allowed to accompany Jesus on His travels. **Jesus granted the first two requests but not the last. Instead, He told the man to return home and become a witness for Him (vv. 19–20). The homeless man was then sent on his way.**

What do you think this passage says about Jesus? Turn your reflections into a prayer asking Him to deliver you from all evil.

Why do you think Jesus granted the first two requests but not the third? How important is being a witness at home and in one's neighborhood? Assess your own testimony in the light of this truth.

Day 16

Read Mark 5:21–43

The previous two passages show Jesus as Lord in control over both nature and demons. This passage shows His lordship over disease and death.

Two people fell at Jesus's feet: Jairus the synagogue ruler (v. 22) and a woman troubled by a chronic and debilitating illness (v. 33).

When Jairus told Jesus about his dying 12-year-old daughter, Jesus compassionately accompanied him back home (vv. 23–24). A large crowd followed. In that crowd was a miserable woman who had suffered from a bleeding illness for 12 years. She had seen many doctors, only to suffer "a great deal," using up all her money and yet getting even worse (v. 26). She secretly touched Jesus's cloak and was healed immediately (vv. 27–29). Women in her condition were ceremonially unclean and not to be touched (Leviticus 15:19–31), but **rituals were no barriers to Jesus and His power to heal.** He felt power going out from Him (Mark 5:30) and stopped to ask who in the crowd had touched Him. Caught "red-handed," the woman fell at His feet and told Him everything. Despite the surging crowd, she managed to actually touch Him. As Augustine writes, "Flesh presses, faith touches." Jesus commended her faith and publicly declared her healed (vv. 33–34).[3] She was the only woman in the Gospels that Jesus addressed as "Daughter" (v. 34). In His compassion and divine kindness, He brought her new dignity.

News then arrived that the little girl had died. Unperturbed, Jesus continued on to the house, reassuring Jairus and encouraging him to believe (v. 36). At the house, mourners were wailing loudly. Jesus told them that the child was only "asleep," to which they responded with laughter (vv. 38–40). Accompanied by the parents and three of His disciples, Jesus went to where the dead child was lying. He took the girl by the hand and said, "Little girl, . . . get up!" (v. 41), and she got up immediately (v. 42). Those present were "completely astonished" (v. 42).

Jesus gave strict orders to keep this miracle a secret—as His time for crucifixion had not arrived, He did not want His fame to spread prematurely. Jesus then asked the parents to "give her something to eat" (v. 43). Besides proving to everyone that the girl's health had been fully restored, this was also a lovely gesture of care and concern from the Lord of compassion. He is not a superstar magician, but the Lord of life who cares for every aspect of our lives.

[3] John Augustus William Haas, *Annotations on the Gospel According to St. Mark*, Vol. 3 (London: Forgotten Books, 2013), 97.

Reflect on the power of the Lord over disease and death. Talk to Him about your own fears of illness and dying.

Jesus was touched by the sick woman and He touched the dead girl. Why is His touch important? What does it convey? What lessons can we learn when ministering to sick and dying people?

Day 17

Read Mark 6:1–6

It is always nice to return home, to friends, family, and familiar surroundings. Jesus returned to Nazareth with His disciples and taught at the synagogue on the Sabbath. Those listening were amazed and asked themselves, "Where did this man get these things?" (v. 2). They had known Him since His childhood days. He did not attend any formal religious school, nor did He study under some famous rabbi. So where had He gained such wisdom? "What's this wisdom that has been given him? What are these remarkable miracles he is performing?" (v. 2). They were clearly impressed with His words and actions.

They could not believe that this was the Jesus they knew, the man who had made many of their tables and chairs, ploughs and other implements. "Isn't this the carpenter?" they asked (v. 3). This was not a compliment. It was like saying, "After all, he is only the village carpenter." The word translated as "carpenter" refers to a skilled workman who built things. "Isn't this Mary's son?" they asked, suggesting either that Joseph had passed away by this time or that this was another subtle insult (usually one was identified as the son of one's father) related to lingering doubts about His parentage. Also, they referred to the siblings of Jesus, who were ordinary folks like everyone else. With these thoughts, they dismissed Jesus, His teachings, and His miracles. They did not believe Him and "took offense at him" (v. 3). They were outraged that this ordinary man among them, or so they thought, was claiming to be a special messenger from God.

Jesus must have been sadly hurt by the rejection of friends and neighbors. "A prophet is not without honor except in his own town, among his relatives and in his own home" (v. 4). Phillip Brooks aptly comments that familiarity breeds contempt "only with contemptible things or among contemptible people."[4] As a result, apart from a few cases of healing, Jesus "could not do any miracles there" (v. 5). God would not entertain unbelief.

It was now Jesus's turn to be amazed (cf. v. 2). He was amazed at their lack of faith (v. 6). On another occasion, Jesus was amazed by the faith of a Gentile centurion (Luke 7:9). **It was the presence or absence of faith that amazed our Lord.**

[4] Daniel L. Akin, *Christ-Centred Exposition Commentary: Exalting Jesus in Mark* (Nashville, Tennessee: Holman, 2014), 122.

Is it possible to become too familiar with Jesus, so much so that we can take Him for granted? What can be done to keep our view of Him fresh?

Jesus is amazed by the presence of faith and the absence of it. In your life, has Jesus been amazed? Why or why not?

Day 18

Read Mark 6:7–13

Not all towns rejected Him like His hometown Nazareth, so Jesus went about teaching in an active itinerant ministry "from village to village" (v. 6). With so much to be done, Jesus gathered His disciples ("Calling the Twelve to him") and "sent them out two by two" to replicate what He was doing (v. 7). He originally gathered the disciples to be with Him and then to preach the good news to others (Mark 3:14). Now it was time for them to take on their first assignment and go out in His Name.

Jesus sent them out in twos. First, according to Old Testament Law, at least two witnesses were needed to verify a matter (Deuteronomy 19:15). Second, two were better than one as they would be able to help and encourage each other (Ecclesiastes 4:9–12). Jesus gave His disciples "authority over impure spirits" (Mark 6:7) so that their ministry would not be hindered by evil forces. He also gave them strict instructions on how they were to conduct their ministry (vv. 8–11).

They were not to carry extra baggage: only a staff and sandals for the journey. No bread, bag, money, or extra tunics. Why such austerity? They were to be focused on their ministry; extra baggage would become a distraction, as is often the case when we spend inordinate time and energy gathering possessions and then worrying over them. Also, God's servants must trust God for their provision (Matthew 10:10). As Hudson Taylor says, "God's work done in God's way will never lack God's supplies."[5]

In every place, they were to stay in one house, and not make superficial social visits from home to home. Here again, the intensity and urgency of their mission was recognised. If the town or village rejected them and their message, they were to "shake the dust" off their feet and leave— moving on to other places that were more receptive (cf. Acts 13:51). This action would be a testimony against those who had rejected the message. Those who rejected Christ would also be rejected by Him (Matthew 10:33; John 12:48).

The disciples faithfully did what Jesus was doing: preaching repentance, exorcising demons, and healing the sick (Mark 6:12–13). **Our ministry is simply a continuation of the ministry of Jesus.**

---

[5] Leslie T. Lyall, *A Passion for the Impossible: The Continuing Story of the Mission Hudson Taylor Began* (London: OMF Books, 1965), 37.

Jesus sent out His disciples two by two. Where has He sent you? Who are your partners in this ministry, and how do you work together? Who do you think had to partner with Judas Iscariot? What would have been his experience?

Why is it important to discard excess baggage when serving Christ? What implications are there for you?

Day 19

Read Mark 6:14–29

The ministry of the Twelve whom Jesus sent out was inspiring. "Jesus' name had become well known" (v. 14), rather than the names of the disciples—an important lesson for the Lord's servants. Herod heard about the ministry too and was filled with fear. With a guilty conscience, he thought that Jesus was John the Baptist, whom he had earlier beheaded (v. 16).

Mark then recounts the sordid tale of John's execution. Herod had married his brother's wife Herodias (vv. 17–18; Luke 3:19–20), and John was arrested after rebuking the king for this sin. Herod had some respect for John and liked to listen to him despite of his barbed messages (v. 20), but Herodias was after John's blood and found an opportunity when Herod threw a grand birthday party for himself. Herodias's daughter danced (inappropriately, many commentators believe) and Herod was so pleased that he offered to give anything she asked (vv. 22–23). With her wicked mother's prompting, the girl asked for John's head.

The proud Herod, not wanting to retract his boastful offer to the girl in front of his guests, chose to kill God's honest and courageous prophet rather than damage his already-frayed reputation. Though "greatly distressed" (v. 26), he ordered the beheading of John. The head was then presented to the evil Herodias. How could God allow His chosen servants to be so easily disposed of by such sinful and small-minded people? Some may ask whether this is how God treats His friends.

When Jesus was told about John's beheading, He "withdrew by boat privately to a solitary place" (Matthew 14:13). He may have wanted to talk to His Father about it and mourn privately for John, who was also His relative (see Luke 1:36). Also, He may have realized that He too would be cruelly put to death. But God's will would be done, and even if it meant suffering, it was more important to die faithfully doing God's will than live on in unfaithfulness. **God will have the final word in all our lives. His justice will prevail regardless of our present predicament.** Even in suffering, the servant can say, "The LORD will fulfill his purpose for me" (Psalm 138:8, ESV). History records that Herod and Herodias eventually fell out of favor with Rome, were banished, and committed suicide.

What do you think God feels when His people are persecuted by powerful forces on earth? What other powers may be behind such persecution? What do you think God does in such situations, and why?

Why is suffering and setbacks so much a part of God's will for our lives? What truths about God help us when we undergo suffering?

Day 20

Read Mark 6:30–44

Apart from the resurrection of Jesus, the miracle of the feeding of the 5,000 is the only one recorded in all four gospels. It has a special place in the memory of the church. The text begins where it left off in Mark 6:13. The disciples returned to Jesus to report "all they had done and taught" (v. 30). It is important to keep returning to Jesus to prevent pride and distractions from leading us astray in our ministry. Given the ever-present crowd, Jesus invited His tired disciples to "Come with me by yourselves to a quiet place and get some rest" (v. 31; cf. Mark 9:30–31). But the crowds followed relentlessly. Jesus felt compassion for them, for they were "like sheep without a shepherd" (v. 34). So He taught them.

Then a massive catering problem arose. It was getting late and the disciples advised Jesus to send the crowd away. Can we forget human need by simply dismissing the needy? Jesus asked the disciples to give the people some food (v. 37). The pragmatic among them made some quick calculations and remarked that it would take eight months' of a man's wages to feed everyone present. They did not realize that Jesus was about to perform a great miracle. When He asked them what food was available, they said there were only five loaves and two fish. In John's account, the sheer impossibility of the situation is conveyed through humor—there was a "great crowd" (John 6:2, 5), a young boy with a few small loaves of bread and some fish (6:9), and "plenty of grass" (6:10).

Yet, by the power of Jesus, it was enough for all. He gave thanks, broke the loaves, and distributed them. "They all ate and were satisfied" (Mark 6:42). Moreover, after the meal, the disciples picked up "twelve basketfuls of broken pieces of bread and fish" (v. 43). In a kind gesture, Jesus provided sufficient supplies for each disciple. While Mark does not explain why Jesus performs the miracle, other than that the people were hungry and in need of physical food, John links this event with the truth that Jesus is the "true bread from heaven" and the "bread of life" (John 6:32–35). **The miracle points us to Jesus, in whom our deepest spiritual hunger is satisfied.**

Why did Jesus invite His tired disciples to go away quietly with Him to rest? How can you do this regularly in your own life?

Jesus stretched the limited resources miraculously. How does God involve us in His miracles? What does it say about God and His methods?

Read Mark 6:45–56

After the great miracle, Jesus sent His disciples across the lake to Bethsaida while He dismissed the crowd and spent time praying alone on a mountainside (vv. 45–46). The growing crowds and the death of John the Baptist had made Jesus long for some solitude in which to pray.

Jesus could see that the disciples on the boat were having a tough time rowing against the strong wind (v. 48). Later, at about 3 a.m. ("the fourth watch"), they were still struggling on the lake, and He went out to them. They saw that He was walking on the water! He was moving faster than they were and had quickly caught up. They were terrified to see someone walking on the water and mistook Him for a ghost (v. 49). Jesus appeared to pass them by (cf. Luke 24:28). Then He spoke to the disciples: "Take courage! It is I. Don't be afraid" (Mark 6:50).

Jesus got into the boat and "the wind died down." The disciples were "completely amazed" (v. 51). "They had not understood about the loaves; their hearts were hardened" (v. 52). This was the reason for their fear and amazement. They didn't seem to have learned from previous experience. Jesus had already calmed a terrible storm once before in Mark 4:35–41 (the same one, perhaps), when He was with them in a boat. Even though this time He was initially outside the boat, no wind or wave could stop Him from getting into it. And they didn't understand the significance of the loaves—if Jesus could miraculously feed such a large crowd, would He not be capable of walking on water and other supernatural things? Had He not already demonstrated that He was the Son of God? They still seem to have harbored doubts and anxieties. **Their hearts were hardened into old ways of thinking and they had difficulty accepting and understanding the new revelation of Christ.**

Did the rest of the journey pass in silence or did Jesus teach them further? We don't know. But when they landed on the shore, "people recognized Jesus" (v. 54) and soon a great crowd thronged around Jesus to be healed—"all who touched [his cloak] were healed" (v. 56). Jesus was at the height of His popularity, but dark clouds were gathering.

Why do you think Jesus needed time alone to pray (v. 46)? Martin Luther observed that the busier we become, the more we need to pray. How is your own prayer life in this regard?

The disciples struggled against the wind, and Jesus helped them in His own time. Reflect on some of the winds that you are presently struggling against as they impede your progress. How do you think Jesus is helping you?

Day 22

Read Mark 7:1–23

The disciples gathered around Jesus (6:30), but so too did His opponents, the Pharisees and teachers of the law (v. 1). One group gathered to report and learn, while the other did so to find fault.

The Pharisees had many man-made traditions "of the elders" (vv. 3, 5), such as ceremonial washing before eating. They asked Jesus why His disciples were eating with (ritually) unwashed, "defiled" hands (v. 5). In their criticism, they were indirectly blaming Jesus for not teaching them properly and for not upholding their traditions.

In His reply, Jesus referred to Scripture, where God had declared in Isaiah 29:13 that the Jews worshiped and honored Him only with their lips but not their hearts, which had grown far away from God— "their teachings are merely human rules" (Mark 7:6–7). Sadly, they only had the right language and not the right life, but **God could see through such hypocrisy.** Jesus accused His opponents of, ironically, abandoning the commands of God in order to champion their own human traditions (v. 8). He illustrated His point by showing how they had used man-made traditions to excuse themselves from following God's laws. Instead of obeying the fifth commandment to honor their parents (vv. 10-12), which often involved providing financial support, they hid behind the tradition of "Corban" (v. 11). Corban referred to "a gift devoted to God," which allowed anyone to declare what they owned as dedicated to God. Once they had done so, they were no longer obligated to give it away, even to their parents. Jesus must have been exasperated by the spiritual blindness and hypocrisy of the religious leaders.

Jesus then "called the crowd to him" (v. 14) and spoke with divine authority. "Listen to me, everyone, and understand this" (v. 14). Three actions were required. To go to Jesus, to listen to Him, and to understand (which included obedience). Against the ritualistic foolishness of the Pharisees, Jesus declared that people were defiled not by what goes in but what comes out (v. 15).

Later His disciples asked Jesus what He meant. Jesus was exasperated and exclaimed, "Are you so dull?" (v. 18). He then said that it was not food (that goes through the alimentary canal) that defiled a man but what came out (through one's speech, thoughts, and actions) from a wicked and sinful heart (vv. 18–23). The problem was not ritually unclean hands but actually defiled hearts. As we read in Isaiah, the problem lay more deeply with the heart than with the lips (29:13). The Pharisees were barking up the wrong tree.

Can you think of a modern example of how the traditions of men are given more importance than the commands of God? How can this be reversed?

How can we come near Jesus, listen to Him, and understand? Think of an example of how you experienced this? Why is the heart important in this process?

Day 23

Read Mark 7:24–30

While Jesus ministered largely in Galilee and Judea, within the traditional borders of Israel, He also ministered in Gentile areas. This time He stepped across the border to the region of Tyre and Sidon, both Gentile cities. He entered a house secretly (v. 24). Why? Was it a Gentile home? As Gentiles were considered unclean, Jews were not to mix with them or enter their houses, lest they too become defiled. If Jesus visited a Gentile home covertly, it meant that He was now breaking down the walls that divided Jew from Gentile, without however creating an unnecessary stumbling block for pious Jews who might have objected to His actions. Later, after He had completed His mission at the cross and when the Spirit had been given to the church, He would guide Peter to do the same—to cross the boundary between Jews and Gentiles with God's inclusive grace (Acts 10:9–48).

A deeply troubled Gentile Syrophoenician woman came to Jesus and fell at His feet, begging Him to drive out a demon from her little daughter (Mark 7:25–26). In His answer (v. 27), Jesus appeared to be rather harsh. He differentiated the Jews ("children") from the Gentiles ("dogs"). Matthew 15:24 elaborates further, stating that Jesus indicated that He was sent "only to the lost sheep of Israel." The Jews considered dogs to be unclean animals and habitually called Gentiles "dogs" in a derogatory sense. It is noteworthy that Jesus did not use the usual slur here, but instead a term meaning "little dogs" (or pet dogs)—William Barclay observes that "Jesus took the sting out of the word."[6]

This was a test for the woman, and she passed with flying colors. She agreed with Jesus, "Yes, Lord." She called Him Lord and included herself as one of His subjects. She added that "even the dogs under the table eat the children's crumbs" (v. 28). She humbly persisted in her supplication. Jesus was greatly impressed with her, and told her: "For such a reply, you may go; the demon has left your daughter" (v. 29). Matthew 15:28 further elaborates on Jesus' response: "Woman, you have great faith! Your request is granted." He commended her for her "great faith" and granted her heartfelt and humble request. Here is an example of exorcism from a distance, underlining the Lord's amazing authority. **The Lord's ministry was now touching the lives of Gentiles**, something that would become clearer and more extensive in the days to come, after He had appointed Paul to be His missionary to the Gentiles (Acts 9:15).

[6] William Barclay, *The Daily Study Bible: The Gospel of Mark*, rev. ed. (Westminster: John Knox Press, 2001), 402–403.

ThinkThrough

God called Abraham to bless him so that all peoples on earth would be blessed through him (Genesis 12:2). Why did the Jews fail to realize that God intended to bless non-Jews too (Isaiah 19:25; 56:6–7)? How did Jesus correct this?

Why did Jesus say that the woman had "great faith"? How does the Lord test us so that we may display such great faith? Can you remember a moment like this in your own experience?

Day 24

Read Mark 7:31–37

Jesus moved on from Tyre and Sidon to another Gentile area, the Decapolis (Ten Cities), east of the Sea of Galilee (v. 31). There a deaf and dumb man was brought to Him by some people who begged Jesus to "place his hand" on the man (v. 32). They may have heard of how the famous healer had healed many people and wished to see the same happen in this man (cf. Mark 5:20). It must be miserable not being able to hear what others wanted or to express what you want.

Jesus took the man away from the crowd, partly to perform a more private healing and partly because of the unusual method He used. He put His fingers into the man's ears and then applied His spit on his tongue (Mark 7:33). Jesus would employ different methods—for it was not the method but the Man that really mattered. Here Jesus did not talk to the man since he was deaf. Rather, He used a method that the man could perceive clearly, that would give him confidence in being healed. Jesus turned His eyes toward heaven and with a deep sigh commanded, "Be opened" (v. 34). The word for "sigh" is also used for the "groans" of the Holy Spirit who intercedes from within us (Romans 8:26). It shows how deeply God feels for us and how much He is involved in our lives.

The man's ears were opened and he could now hear. His tongue was loosened. The Greek word (*mogilalon*) translated "tongue" is a rare word found only here in the New Testament. It more accurately means "impediment in speech." It is used also once in the Septuagint (the Greek translation of the Hebrew Bible) in Isaiah 35:5–6 where the Messiah is said to loosen tongues and open ears. Mark indicates by the use of this rare word that Jesus is that Messiah.

Again, Jesus is careful not to publicize this event—because His time to die had not yet come. But "overwhelmed with amazement," the people could not keep what they saw to themselves. It was too amazing not to share. They spoke highly of Jesus: "He has done everything well" (Mark 7:37). **The Creator who pronounced all He had created "very good" (Genesis 1:31) would now re-create His new kingdom, excellently.**

Jesus sighed deeply as He turned to His Father in prayer. What do you think was communicated and expressed through that sigh? What does it say about how close Jesus is to us in our troubles?

Jesus did everything well. Think of situations in your past (or present) when you felt doubts about Jesus's care for you or His wisdom and ability to help you. Why did you think so? How can you deal with such doubts?

Day 25

Read Mark 8:1–13

Here was "another large crowd" (v. 1). Jesus taught with such amazing authority, freshness, and relevance that the people stayed on for three days. By then they had run out of food and were hungry. Jesus, as He always did, felt compassion for them (v. 2), and was concerned that some would collapse on the way home (v. 3).

Instead of saying, "Lord you miraculously fed the 5,000. You can do it now too," the disciples pointed out that they were in a remote place and it was impossible to feed such a crowd (v. 4). How could they have forgotten the recent miracle? **It is easy when facing present challenges to forget past expressions of God's faithfulness and power.** The faith of the disciples was at a depressing low.

Patiently, Jesus asked them how many loaves they had. This time they offered from their own supplies seven loaves (v. 5). In the same way as previously, Jesus gave thanks, broke the bread, and distributed it, thus miraculously feeding the hungry and grateful crowd (vv. 6–7). The disciples later contributed "a few small fish" (v. 7) too. Perhaps they held back the fish to see what Jesus would do with the loaves first—like the way we often hold back from giving Him everything we have, just in case. The people were asked to sit, for it was going to be a full meal. "The people ate and were satisfied" (v. 8). After the meal, the disciples "picked up seven basketfuls of broken pieces" (v. 8).

After Jesus and His disciples returned to Jewish territory, they went to the region of Dalmanutha, where they were approached by Pharisees who came to test Jesus with more questions. The word for "test" can also be translated as "tempt," for we can see Satan's diabolical suggestions (cf. Matthew 4:5–7) behind the Pharisees' demand for a miraculous sign from heaven (Mark 8:11) to prove that Jesus's power came from God, not Satan. Jesus "sighed deeply" at their stubborn unbelief and refused to perform any such miracle (v. 12)—He had already done enough to prove His identity. The Pharisees were not seriously looking for a sign, and Jesus refused to be their resident magician.

How often do we forget the wonderful acts of God in the past in answer to our prayers? Why do we forget so easily when faced with a present crisis? What lessons can we learn from Jesus's response to such lack of faith?

Why did Jesus refuse to perform additional miracles for the Pharisees? In what way was it a temptation? What kind of faith does Jesus look for?

Day 26

Read Mark 8:14–21

In the wake of the previous passage (feeding of the 4,000), there is a continuing discussion on bread. Jesus warned the disciples about the "yeast of the Pharisees and that of Herod" (v. 15). Clueless as to what He meant, the disciples discussed among themselves and decided He was talking about their present lack of bread (v. 16).

Jesus seemed exasperated by their lack of understanding—what a bunch of dim-witted disciples! "Do you still not see or understand? Are your hearts hardened?" (v. 17). Jesus remarked sadly that they had unseeing eyes and unhearing ears (v. 18). He then reminded them about the two miracles of feeding the crowds (vv. 19–20). In each case, He asked them how many baskets of leftover pieces they had collected. Their answer was arithmetically correct but its significance still eluded them. Further exasperated, Jesus asked, "Do you still not understand?" (v. 21).

What did the disciples fail to understand? When Jesus mentioned yeast, they should have remembered the trick of mixing a pinch of old, yeast-rich dough in with a new batch to help it rise. While this is helpful practice in the kitchen, in this case Jesus used it to point out the harmful effects of putting the "old dough" of the Pharisees into the new teaching of Jesus. Here, yeast was used by Jesus to represent the sinfulness of the human heart, which was abundantly found in the false piety of the Pharisees. They had totally misunderstood the nature of the kingdom of God and considered it only in terms of power and ritual. The Herodians were even worse, focusing on political power and expediency. These remain dangerous and pervasive influences. Jesus warned the disciples against ever giving ear to these false versions of the kingdom of God.

But the disciples were so focused on their lack of physical bread that spiritual lessons from the Master degenerated into materialistic concerns in their hearts. The key words are "forgotten" (v. 14) and "remember" (v. 18). The disciples forgot to bring bread for the journey—that was their carelessness. But they also failed to remember the lesson of the feeding miracles—that Jesus who fed crowds would have no problem feeding His disciples. Rather, they should have trusted Jesus and listened to the deep spiritual truths He was teaching. They were forgetful and distracted students, and slow to understand.

ThinkThrough

Read the words of Jesus to His disciples in verses 17–18 and 21. Imagine the tone with which Jesus said those words. Was there, anger, frustration, concern, love? Can you remember any such communication between Jesus and you?

Read Matthew 6:31–34. When we are distracted by "survival" concerns (what to eat and wear, how to pay for things, and so on), how does such preoccupation prevent us from receiving "real life" lessons from Jesus? Turn your thoughts into prayer.

Day 27

Read Mark 8:22–26

People kept bringing the sick to Jesus. This time some "brought a blind man and begged Jesus to touch him" (v. 22). We are likewise reminded to bring the sick to Jesus in earnest prayer. Jesus held the blind man's hand and brought him outside the village—for some privacy. Jesus was careful not to let His fame spread ahead of His timing for the cross.

Again in an unusual way, Jesus spat on the man's eyes and put His hands on him and asked whether he saw anything (v. 23). It appears that he was healed partially, for he could see people but they looked "like trees walking around" (v. 24). Then Jesus touched the man's eyes again. This time there was a complete healing. Mark uses various phrases to emphasise this: a) "his eyes were opened," b) "his sight was restored," and c) "he saw everything clearly" (v. 25).

Why did Jesus use this "two-step" healing method? Was this a difficult case? Or was Jesus trying to teach something? At times, we need healing even after the first touch. When Jonah, the Old Testament prophet, preached in Nineveh and received an astounding response when the whole city repented, he sulked outside the city gates hoping that God would change His mind and wipe out this enemy of Israel. Jonah responded strongly when a vine grew above him to give shade and also when the vine withered. But he failed to be deeply moved by the condition of the city's people and their future. God told him, "You have been concerned about this plant . . . should I not have concern for the great city of Nineveh?" (Jonah 4:10–11). Jonah had a problem with his spiritual eyesight. He could not tell the difference between a vine and a city. He needed a second touch from God to help him see clearly. **Likewise, we are often in need of a second touch from Jesus.**

Why did Jesus ask the man not to go into the village (Mark 8:26)? Some manuscripts have the words "Don't go and tell anyone in the village." Again, Jesus was not keen on publicizing Himself at this time. People still had wrong ideas about who He was. A time would come when He would be better understood and, after the cross, He would be widely made known.

Why do you think Jesus was reticent about making Himself known widely? Is this still true today, or are we to openly make Him known? What about some modern preachers who seek personal fame?

Jesus asked, "Do you see anything?" If He were to ask you the same question, what would be your answer? Where do you think you would need a second touch from Him?

Day 28

Read Mark 8:27–30

With His unparalleled, authoritative teaching and His amazing miracles, Jesus was the talk of the town. His fame spread throughout the land, and people had all kinds of theories about Him.

Continuing His itinerant ministry, Jesus brought His disciples to the far north of the country, to Caesarea Philippi, a city with many pagan worship sites. Jesus then asked His disciples, "Who do people say I am?" (v. 27). They told Him some of the popular speculation about His identity. Some had said He was John the Baptist—or that at least the spirit of John was in Him. Others said He was Elijah who had returned to earth; Elijah had been taken up to heaven and did not appear to have died (2 Kings 2:11–12). Yet others suggested that He might be one of the prophets.

Jesus then turned the question around. "But what about you? Who do you say I am?" (Mark 8:29). It was obvious that none of the theories they had heard was acceptable. Jesus wanted to know who they thought He was. It's like something a professor would ask if his student's term paper is merely a collation of what others have written, "What do you yourself think?" The disciples must have paused for thought, but Peter, in his usual impulsive way, was first off with a brilliant answer. "You are the Messiah" (v. 29). Messiah is Hebrew for "The Anointed One," the Greek "Christ." That Jesus was pleased with Peter's answer is shown in Matthew when Jesus replied, "Blessed are you, Simon son of Jonah, for this was not revealed to you by flesh and blood, but by my Father in heaven" (Matthew 16:17). **What Peter had said did not come from popular surveys, but from heaven. It was not social opinion but divine revelation.** Peter's confession of Jesus's identity is the unshakeable rock of the church, and no satanic attack can overcome a church built on this rock (Matthew 16:18–19).

Again, Jesus warned His disciples to keep this revelation a secret—not forever, but "until the Son of Man had risen from the dead" (Mark 9:9). The secrecy was only temporary, until all the things said about Jesus would be fulfilled. Then the whole world would be told (16:15).

ThinkThrough

If Jesus were to ask you the question He asked the disciples, what would be your answer? Turn your answer to prayer, thanking Him for who He is and what He has done for you.

Reflect on how your profession of faith is actually shown in your daily practice—in your thoughts, attitudes, speech, actions, relationships, priorities, and habits.

Read Mark 8:31–

After Peter was commended for declaring the revealed truth about Jesus, the Lord then taught that He "must suffer many things" (v. 31). It must have disturbed the disciples to learn that their Messiah would have to suffer. Would not the Messiah be strong and victorious? Why was Jesus talking about suffering? Their beloved Teacher suffering? Surely not! As they reeled from what He had just said, Jesus gave further details. He will be rejected by the leaders and killed, but He will rise again after three days (v. 31). "He spoke plainly about this" (v. 32)—He was not speaking symbolically. All this will happen because of human sin and God's love.

Peter could not take it anymore and "took him aside and began to rebuke him" (v. 32). Imagine that: Peter rebuking Jesus! Peter was convinced that the Messiah would ascend a throne, not hang on a cross. He must have chided Jesus for talking like a defeated man. Jesus then rebuked Peter: "Get behind me Satan! . . . You do not have in mind the concerns of God, but merely human concerns" (v. 33). He who, only a while ago, was commended for speaking what heaven had revealed had now given ear to Satan's whispers and the chatter of men. How easy to fall like this!

Peter was like the blind man of Bethsaida who could only see partially for a while; he needed a second touch. He may have had sight but lacked insight. **Jesus then made clear the ways of His kingdom—it was the way of the cross. Anyone who sought to follow Christ must "deny themselves and take up their cross" (v. 34).** Jesus then stated some related principles. We gain eternal life by losing our earthly lives for Christ (v. 35). Weighed against all that the world offers is the value of one's soul (vv. 36–37). If a disciple is ashamed of Jesus in an ungodly world, Jesus will be ashamed of him when He returns (v. 38).

This may have sounded rather depressing to the disciples, who were expecting the kingdom to come about in a different way. But Jesus assured them that some among the crowd would see the kingdom of God come with power—which prepares three disciples for the Transfiguration experience (Mark 9:2–8). Dark clouds were gathering, but bright sunshine lay beyond them.

Read Isaiah 52:13–53:12. Why must the Messiah be also the Suffering Servant? Why did the disciples have difficulty understanding this? How does the truth of the Suffering Messiah help you in your walk with Him?

What satanic whispers and human chatter exist today to distort the truth about Jesus? How would you correct them? Consider the principles of following Christ that Jesus taught.

Read Mark 9:2–13

After the depressing darkness of what Jesus had told them—that He would suffer and those who follow Him must as well—Jesus took Peter, James, and John (the inner circle) up a high mountain for an extraordinary experience (v. 2). What Mark writes here would have been from Peter's eyewitness account (cf. 2 Peter 1:16–18). Jesus was transfigured, a glory that came from His sinless nature (Mark 9:3) and sonship (v. 7). His clothes were dazzling white, whiter than any earthly bleach could achieve (v. 3). Elsewhere we read that His face also "shone like the sun" (Matthew 17:2). The curtain was temporarily lifted to reveal Jesus as He really was—in all His heavenly glory. This was to reassure the disciples that the cross was on the road to glory, that Jesus knew what He was doing.

Moses and Elijah, representing the Law and the Prophets (Old Testament) appeared and talked to Jesus to whom the Old Testament points (cf. Luke 24:27). They were speaking about "his departure" (Luke 9:31). Peter, who was asleep with the others (Luke 9:32; they tended to sleep whenever Jesus invited them to special experiences; cf. Mark 14:37–41), woke up astounded and blurted something about building three shelters for the glorified figures. He spoke out of fear and confusion (Mark 9:6). His errors were that he apparently interrupted the conversation between Jesus and the other two, put Jesus on the same platform with Moses and Elijah, and perhaps rejoiced with relief that dwelling permanently in the glory would put away any idea of the cross.

But the heavenly Father, speaking from a cloud, interrupted Peter and told the disciples that Jesus is His incomparable Son and that they must listen to Him (v. 7). Suddenly, only Jesus was left standing there.

Then they came down the mountain. The cross still awaited Jesus. Jesus cautioned them to keep the matter to themselves until the resurrection (v. 9), for reasons already mentioned earlier. They then asked about the teaching that Elijah must precede the coming of the Messiah. Jesus replied that Elijah (John the Baptist) had already come (vv. 11–13).

What Peter saw on the mountain remained with him for the rest of his life. Much later he would write about it (2 Peter 1:16–18). That view of the glorified Jesus sustained him amid all kinds of suffering, even death.

ThinkThrough

Read Revelation 1:12–20. John had another vision of the glorified Jesus. Why was this necessary before he began describing the suffering and persecution that the church would face till Christ returned? How does the glory of God help us to bear the cross?

The Father commands us to listen to His Son. How have you been listening to Jesus lately? Take time to listen to what He is saying to you.

Day 31

Read Mark 9:14–32

How different the noisy and messy plains were from the dignified scene on the glorious mountain! Campbell Morgan wrote, "He found disputing scribes, a distracted father, a demon-possessed boy, and defeated disciples . . . He silenced the scribes, He comforted the father, He healed the boy, He instructed the disciples."[7] The scribes were arguing with the other disciples because of their inability to exorcise the demon that had caused the boy to be mute. In desperate tones, the father told Jesus about how his son had suffered from childhood. The evil spirit caused fit-like symptoms and often threw the boy into fire or water in order to kill him (vv. 17–22). It was a helpless situation.

Jesus was disappointed when he said, "You unbelieving generation" (v. 19). Was He speaking about the scribes, the disciples, the father, the crowd, or all of them? The problem was lack of faith. The father told Jesus "if you can do anything, take pity on us" (v. 22). Jesus corrected him by saying that the issue was not the power of Jesus but whether the man had faith (v. 23). The man replied with an honest prayer. "I do believe; help me overcome my unbelief! (v. 24). He knew that he had faith but it was also deficient.

Jesus then delivered the boy from the vicious demon. He knew it was a "deaf and mute spirit" (v. 25) and forbade it to return. Jesus took the boy by the hand and lifted him to his feet (v. 27). How kind and gentle of Jesus! The boy's father must have been greatly relieved that what had troubled his family was now gone. The disciples were astounded and the scribes were silenced.

Later, in private, as they would often do, the disciples sought further explanation from Jesus. They asked Him why they could not drive out the evil spirit (v. 28). After all, Jesus had given them authority over demons (Mark 6:7). Jesus answered that this particular kind of spirit (perhaps higher up in the demonic hierarchy) "can come out only by prayer" (9:29). Some manuscripts have the phrase "prayer and fasting." **As Warren Wiersbe wrote, "faith must be cultivated through spiritual discipline and devotion."[8] Authority is not just a gift but a fruit from within a totally committed heart.**

[7] G. Campbell Morgan, *The Gospel According to Mark* (New York: Fleming H. Revell Company, 1927), 194.

[8] Warren Wiersbe, *Be Diligent: Serving Others as You Walk with the Master Servant* (Colorado Springs: David C. Cook, 2010), 109.

ThinkThrough

How does belief mix with unbelief? To what extent has faith to do with what you know about Jesus and how much you trust Him? Turn your thoughts into prayer.

Jesus took time to teach and train His disciples and gave it priority (vv. 30–31). Why do you think this was necessary? How can our time with important people in our lives (family, colleagues, and mentees) be threatened by the constant demands on our time from other urgent matters?

Day 32

Read Mark 9:33–37

It must have taken some time to return to Capernaum, the base of Jesus's ministry in Galilee. On the way, the disciples engaged in their favorite conversation topic: who the greatest among them should be (vv. 33–34). Still harboring hopes about the glorious kingdom that Jesus the Messiah would bring about on earth, they were already vying for key positions in that kingdom. But although they whispered among themselves, Jesus knew what they were thinking.

Jesus sat down (meaning He was about to teach them) and explained to them what true greatness was. "Anyone who wants to be first must be the very last, and the servant of all" (v. 35). Jesus himself demonstrated this. He was the greatest in the kingdom and "the Father had put all things under his power"; yet He served His disciples by washing their dirty feet (John 13:3–5). Even "the Son of Man did not come to be served, but to serve" (Mark 10:45).

In His kingdom, Jesus expects His disciples to seek to be last ("the very last"; v. 35) rather than first, to be servant rather than ruler of all.

This goes against the grain, for in this sinful world people want to be first and to be served. Despite the popularity of "servant leadership" the sinful human heart still desires to be first rather than last. This can be seen often enough, unfortunately, even in church. John writes in his epistle about a church leader, Diotrephes, "who loves to be first" (3 John 1:9). **In the kingdom of God, the sinful ambition to rule must be transformed to the holy ambition to serve.**

Jesus then took a little child in His arms and said that whoever welcomed a child like this was actually welcoming Him and therefore also His Father (Mark 9:37). It is remarkable that Jesus dignified the little child by saying that he or she represented the Father and the Son. What a lesson for the officious disciples, who considered children "nobodies" and chased away them from Jesus (10:13). Demons harmed little children (9:17–22), but in God's hands they were safe and loved. They may have been "nobodies," but they represent how disciples should consider themselves.

Why is it in human nature that people want to be greater than others? What are they looking for, or what authentic need are they trying to meet wrongly?

In practice, assess your own attitudes in life and ministry based on this teaching of Jesus. How can you model your life after Him? As you need the power of the Holy Spirit to live in this way, turn your thoughts into prayer.

Day 33

We often do not allow God's Word to sink deeply into our hearts. Jesus had just spoken about true greatness in His kingdom. What John said to Jesus shows that he was still stuck in worldly ways of thinking. He told Jesus that they saw a man driving out demons (v. 38). This man could have been a disciple of John the Baptist or one of the 72 disciples. The recent failure to drive out a demon on the part of the disciples was an embarrassment and to see others doing so (presumably successfully) would have filled the disciples with "professional envy." They therefore told the man to stop. The reason for their action was: "he was not one of us" (v. 38). Such cliquish thinking would prove harmful in the kingdom.

Jesus therefore corrected John by saying "Do not stop him" (v. 39). The man was casting out demons in the name of Jesus. Jesus reminded John about it, and asked how a man doing ministry in His name could speak ill about Jesus, "for whoever is not against us is for us" (v. 40). **The disciples thought "whoever is not with us is against us," but Jesus corrected that false assumption. He asks for a larger heart than a narrow exclusiveness.** After all, what unites Christians is not "us" but "His name." Christian community is more than a social reality. It is divine community centered on Jesus. It is He and His will that should unite us.

Jesus then develops the theme of what we do in His name. It represents His person and character. The unnamed man was casting out demons in His name. Surely that would be noted by God. But even the simplest actions done in Jesus's name would not go unnoticed by God. Jesus told the truth that "anyone who gives you a cup of water in my name because you belong to the Messiah will certainly not lose their reward" (v. 41). The disciples knew they belonged to Jesus, but they were not sure about the other man. But Jesus urges them to be more generous in their thinking, arguing that even if the man simply gave them a cup of water in His name, he would be recognized and rewarded by God—how much more so, when he was casting out demons in Jesus's name?

What often causes divisions in the church? How much does jealousy, pride, and cliquishness (he is not one of us) feature in church divisions? What lessons can we learn from Jesus?

What does doing something in Jesus's name mean? What would it involve? Reflect on all that you are doing in His name. What is the difference between doing something in His name and some other name, including our own?

Read Mark 9:42–50

I f anyone gave the disciples ("you," v. 41) a cup of water, he would be rewarded, but if he caused "one of these little ones—those who believe in me—to stumble," he would be severely punished (v. 42). The "little ones" referred to the disciples and to all who would follow Jesus. To illustrate, the little child (vv. 36–37) was probably still there. Woe to anyone who would mislead vulnerable disciples, such as the little child and other new converts.

It would be better for them to be thrown into the sea with a large millstone (these were used to grind grain with the help of a donkey, unlike the smaller versions used in the kitchen) tied around the neck (v. 42), which would result in physical death. To be thrown into hell would be a far worse experience.

Jesus then turned the disciples' attention from rewards to sacrifice. It is better to sacrifice a sinning hand or foot or eye than to go to hell with it (vv. 43–47). The striking instruction to cut off hands and feet or to pluck off eyes is not to be taken literally. One can still sin without a hand, foot, or eye if the root of sin is not dealt with. The imagery points to the necessity of self-denial—of not offering parts of one's body to sin (Romans 6:13). One must deny the sinning part its sinful tendencies. The antidote to the sinning parts is to sacrifice the whole self to God (Romans 6:13) as a living sacrifice (12:1). **Every part must be consecrated to God. It is better to sacrifice temporary pleasure for future glory than to give in to temptation and suffer eternally for it.**

Jesus quoted Isaiah 66:24 (the last verse in that book) to describe hell (Mark 9:48). The metaphors used emphasize eternal punishment in hell. Jesus then taught that "everyone will be salted with fire" (v. 49). In the Old Testament, salt was added to sacrifices (Leviticus 2:13). Fire represents the purifying of our faith (cf. 1 Peter 1:7) and salt probably represents the trials and testing added through suffering and persecution. Suffering would be an essential part of discipleship (to make us holy) and we must be prepared to sacrifice anything, even our lives, in order to remain faithful to the Lord. We must remain "salty" (Mark 9:50)—which would result in peace—for us and others.

ThinkThrough

Read Matthew 23:15. How can new converts be dangerously led astray? Is this happening today? What can you do about it?

How can you consecrate each part of your body and life to Jesus? How can you deny yourself when you are tempted to sin?

Day 35

Read Mark 10:1–12

The crowds kept following Jesus, and He continued to teach them (v. 1). The Pharisees approached Jesus to test Him again; they were relentlessly hounding Jesus. They asked Him whether it was lawful for a man to divorce his wife (v. 2). This was a tricky question for there were contending schools of thought among Jewish rabbis. It was true that the Mosaic Law allowed for divorce (Deuteronomy 24:1–4), but there were various interpretations and applications. The more liberal view (following Rabbi Hillel) was that a man was free to divorce his wife for almost any reason, even when a meal was accidentally burned. However, Rabbi Shammai permitted divorce only on the grounds of immorality. His more conservative view was understandably less popular. Instead of taking sides with a particular rabbinic school, Jesus turned their attention inwards and backwards.

The provision for divorce had been made because of human sinfulness ("your hearts were hard"; Mark 10:5). "You should search your hearts to discover the answer to your question. Do you harbor sinful motives?" Jesus seemed to be saying.

Also, Jesus pointed to the creation account in Genesis. God made Adam and Eve and joined them together in marriage, as one flesh. "Therefore what God has joined together, let no one separate" (v. 9). Marriage was for life (1 Corinthians 7:39) and God hated divorce (Malachi 2:16). It was not to be treated lightly.

Later, Jesus explained to His disciples that because marriage was a lifelong, one-flesh union, divorce (other than for unfaithfulness on the part of one spouse, see Matthew 19:9) would lead to adultery when remarriage took place (Mark 10:11–12) because in the eyes of God, the couple was still married. Here, putting all the gospel teachings together, Jesus established that divorce other than for marital unfaithfulness was unacceptable. This was the view of the Reformers in the 16th century. In this case, both parties would be guilty of adultery if they were to remarry. In the case of marital unfaithfulness, the guilty party had already committed adultery; the marriage covenant had already been breached. If a divorce took place, the other spouse was free to remarry. Some also refer to Paul's additional provision for desertion (1 Corinthians 7:15). **Jesus rejected popular forms of easy divorce, which were abuses of the law. Marriage is intended to be for life.**

ThinkThrough

Marriage is God's idea. What do you think is the purpose of marriage? Why is adultery contrary to the purposes of marriage?

How does God respond to failure in marriage? What is the place of sin and grace in marriage?

Read Mark 10:13–16

Parents want the best for their children, and what parent would not want Jesus to bless their children? Many parents brought their children to Jesus "for him to place his hands on them" (v. 13). But the disciples, who were trying to manage their Master's workload, felt that He had no time for such unimportant creatures as little children. It was a culture that treated children as insignificant, and there were people who treated them as less than human. "Children are to be seen but not heard" is a relatively modern adage that reflects attitudes passed on from much older societies.

The problem was that the disciples did not even try to refuse the parents courteously, "We are sorry. The Rabbi is busy with more important things and has no time to attend to the children." Instead they "rebuked" the parents (v. 13); the disciples scolded them in no uncertain terms for wasting Jesus's time. I am reminded of the time when I had to join a long queue at the Church of the Holy Sepulchre in Jerusalem to see the tomb where Jesus was buried and from which He resurrected. Those who were regulating the crowd spoke roughly to the people and even scolded some, and the sanctity of the moment was spoiled by their roughshod manners.

Jesus was "indignant" when He saw the disciples treat the parents and their children badly. He reversed the disciples' insensitive instructions by saying, "Let the little children come to me, and do not hinder them, for the kingdom of God belongs to such as these" (v. 14). He welcomed the children and reproved the disciples for turning them away. He further taught that the kingdom of God belonged to people who were like the little children—innocent and humble. **Jesus elevated the humanity and dignity of little children by using them as a standard for the kingdom of God.** Anyone "who will not receive the kingdom of God like a little child will never enter it" (v. 15). The words must have jolted both disciples and parents.

Jesus then took "the children in his arms, placed his hands on them and blessed them" (v. 16). We note the three actions here. They show the special tenderness of God for children.

ThinkThrough

Why did Jesus say that no one can enter the kingdom of God unless he receives it like a little child? In what way is this true (cf. childlikeness) and how can it be misunderstood (cf. childishness)? How may it be related to the need to be born again (John 3:3)?

What does Jesus teach us in the way we should notice children and minister tenderly to them? How can we do this in the church and in wider society?

Day 37

Read Mark 10:17–31

After ministering to little children, Jesus ministered to a young man (Matthew 19:20) who was already very wealthy (Mark 10:22), perhaps like young entrepreneurs today who become millionaires in their twenties. Or perhaps he was born into a rich family. He ran up to Jesus (with youthful energy and passion) and fell on his knees (with humility and appropriate respect), according to verse 17. Observers would have been impressed. What a fine young man.

He asked Jesus, "Good teacher, what must I do to inherit eternal life?" (v. 17). With every action and word, he appeared even more promising. Jesus pointed to the second section of the Ten Commandments (v. 19), and the young man responded, "all these I have kept since I was a boy" (v. 20). Very impressive indeed! Jesus looked at him lovingly, for he was a nice, intense young man. So Jesus told him the truth. "One thing you lack" (v. 21). The young man had everything going for him. He was rich, humble, and earnestly kept the commandments. What could he lack?

He lacked the most important thing—love for God. Jesus gave him five actions to perform—go, sell, give, come, follow (v. 21). Tragically, he was not willing to do one necessary thing—to release his grip on his wealth and grasp the hand that God extended to him. His "face fell" and he "went away sad" (v. 22). What a miserable young man, who threw away eternal blessings for temporary earthly riches. Jesus told His disciples that it was difficult for the rich to enter the kingdom of God (cf. 1 Timothy 6:9–10), more difficult than "for a camel to go through the eye of a needle" (Mark 10:23–25). But it was not impossible, for "all things are possible with God" (v. 27). Remember Zacchaeus, Joseph of Arimathea, Barnabas, and other rich people who had been converted?

Contrasting himself with the foolish young man, Peter reminded Jesus of how he and the other disciples had left everything to follow Jesus. Jesus commended the disciples and said they had already received many blessings in return and will receive many more in the age to come (vv. 28–30). **God is no one's debtor. Those who are first (preeminent) in this world may end up last in the kingdom, and vice versa (v. 31).**

Why is it difficult for the rich to enter the kingdom of God? Are there any other strong obstacles that prevent people from following Jesus? Think of some of your friends in such situations and pray for them.

What consolation and encouragement is there for those who trust Jesus enough to let go of things they cannot keep to gain what they cannot lose (Jim Elliot)? Is Jesus pointing out to you the one thing you lack?

Day 38

Read Mark 10:32–45

After watching the rich young man walk away and hearing Jesus's disturbing words, the disciples were "astonished" and "afraid" (v. 32). It is not clear why they were astonished and afraid, but perhaps they suspected trouble ahead, in view of some things that Jesus had said earlier. Yet Jesus resolutely set out for Jerusalem with His disciples. He told the Twelve about how He would suffer and die (vv. 33–34)—the third such revelation (cf. Mark 8:31–32; 9:31). This time Jesus gave seven terrifying details about His death: He would be betrayed, condemned, handed over to the Romans, mocked, spat upon, flogged, and killed. The disciples did not understand how their Master could end up being treated this way. Unbelievable! Was Jesus referring to some deeper spiritual truth? He went on to say that He would rise from the dead.

In the ensuing conversation, we can clearly see that the disciples did not understand Jesus (cf. Mark 9:32). James and John, the sons of Zebedee, made a bold request: "we want you to do for us whatever we ask" (10:35). They wanted special seats, immediately to the right and left of Jesus in His glorious kingdom (v. 37). Jesus must have shaken His head at their ignorant and presumptuous request. They were thinking only of earthly power and glory. Like many of us when we ask blessings from God, they did not know what they were asking (v. 37). Jesus then turned their thoughts again to the cross by referring to the cup He had to drink and a baptism (of fire) He had to undergo (v. 38). Jesus refused to grant their selfish request but told them that they would in fact have a share in His sufferings. But they did not understand.

Meanwhile, the other disciples displayed similar ignorance when they got upset with the two brothers (v. 41). Jesus pointed out how foolish and worldly they were. **Worldly people want power and authority to lord over others, but in the kingdom, greatness is measured by humility of service.** The one who "wants to be first must be slave of all" (v. 44). They must learn from the Son of Man himself. Again, Jesus pointed to the cross when He said He would "give his life as a ransom for many."

Later, when John saw the two thieves crucified on the right and left of Jesus (Luke 23:33; for John's presence at the crucifixion, see John 19:26–27), he may have remembered his foolish request and how Jesus had answered him and his brother. Now he finally understood.

ThinkThrough

Why does God not grant many of our prayer requests? Consider some of your requests made to God that on hindsight you now consider to have been made foolishly and ignorantly?

What implications do Jesus's teachings on true greatness and service have on your life and the many relationships you have—at home, the workplace, at church, and around the neighborhood?

Day 39

Read Mark 10:46–52

Jesus and His disciples were on their way to Jerusalem. Like many pilgrims, they had to pass through Jericho before climbing up to the holy city. Knowing that He was to be sacrificed, Jesus was "leading the way" (v. 32) with incredible courage and commitment to His Father's will. In Jericho, Bartimaeus, a blind beggar, was sitting by the roadside. A large crowd passed by, and Bartimaeus heard them excitedly talking about Jesus walking with them. They referred to the Lord as "Jesus of Nazareth" (v. 47), which said little more than His place of origin; Jesus was a common name.

But blind Bartimaeus saw something that the crowd failed to see. He shouted, "Jesus, Son of David, have mercy on me!" (v. 47). How did he know that Jesus was the Son of David? One thing we can be sure of: He knew that the Messiah would be the Son of David, as prophesied in Scripture (2 Samuel 7:14–16). In addressing Jesus that way, the man expressed his faith in Jesus's identity. Jesus responded to his faith by stopping and asking that Bartimaeus be brought to Him (Mark 10:49). Bartimaeus responded most enthusiastically by jumping up, throwing away his cloak (used for begging and sleeping), and coming to Jesus (v. 50). Jesus asked the same question He had asked John and James earlier (v. 36), and the man replied simply, "I want to see" (v. 51).

Jesus healed him by saying simply, "Go, your faith has healed you" (v. 52). The faith he had demonstrated in Jesus's identity became the reason for his healing. Jesus acted as the Messiah in his life and restored his blind eyes. He no longer needed to live as a poor beggar. His eyes clearly seeing, Bartimaeus now "followed Jesus along the road" (v. 52), the road that led to Jerusalem. There he must have seen the triumphant procession of Jesus into the city, and the crucifixion of Jesus. Who knows— he may have seen the risen Christ or the empty tomb. **The crowd had physical sight but no spiritual insight. Bartimaeus had no sight but had deep insight.** Jesus granted his request and blessed him by allowing him to witness such wondrous events and to know that his faith-filled insight was indeed true.

If Jesus were to ask you, "What do you want me to do for you?" what would you say to Him? Turn your answer to prayer.

Bartimaeus had more insight than the crowd. Jesus blessed him to see things that many failed to see. Read the events surrounding the passion, death, and resurrection of Jesus, and ask Jesus to open your eyes to see what you may have failed to see before.

Day 40

Read Mark 11:1–11

Jesus entered Jerusalem in the triumphal procession of the Messiah King, as prophesied in Scripture (Psalm 118:25–26) the jubilant crowds entering Jerusalem shouted in song (Mark 11:9–10). The city had many gates, and the gate nearest the Mount of Olives, through which Jesus entered the city, was the East or Golden Gate. Today it is covered up and locked, as the Jews continue to await the coming of their Messiah (Ezekiel 44:1–3), refusing to believe that He already passed through it some 2,000 years ago.

A colt of a donkey in a nearby village, that "no one has ever ridden," was recruited for the occasion; Jesus sent two of His disciples to get the donkey (Mark 11:2). We wonder what their conversation was along the way. Most of the time, if not always, Jesus walked when traveling. Why a donkey this time? It had been prophesied in Zechariah 9:9. This donkey was given the unique privilege of carrying Jesus on its back. It is interesting to note that some donkey breeds have hair on the back in the shape of a cross. Surely they remind us of this humble donkey which carried Jesus into the holy city. The owners of the donkey questioned the disciples who were untying it for the Master's use (Luke 19:33). When they said, "The Lord needs it," the villagers released the donkey for its sacred task (Mark 11:3–6).

The crowd was elated. So were the disciples. They may have thought of Jesus as the powerful political Messiah who would free His people from the iron yoke of the Romans. **They failed to realize that Jesus was not a political Messiah, but truly the Messiah who came from heaven to seek and save His lost people.** If they had noticed that Jesus did not go to the palace but to the temple in the city, they might have realized His true identity and mission.

Jesus went to the temple and "looked around at everything" (v. 11). He noted all the abuse and unfaithfulness going on in the temple, and on the next day He would respond appropriately. But for now, He returned to Bethany with His disciples, who were probably excited by all they had seen and anticipating glory and greatness, not realizing that the clouds were gathering around Jesus.

It is possible to take part in a joyful religious event and still miss the point. Why do people misunderstand what God is doing? How does ignorance of God's Word contribute to such misunderstanding?

We are the temple of God (1 Corinthians 3:16; 6:19). When Jesus enters our hearts, what would He observe as He looks around at every-thing? Let Him speak to you and respond to Him in prayer.

Day 41

Read Mark 11:12–26

Having observed all that was happening in the temple (v. 11), Jesus returned the next day. He went to the most public area, known as the Court of the Gentiles, where a roaring trade was going on. The temple authorities had allowed such business—and gained from it. "Approved" animals for temple sacrifices were only sold in the temple. The money changers were busy making huge profits—special temple currency had to be used to buy the animals and to pay the temple tax (v. 15). Aflame with passion for God's name and glory, Jesus drove away the entire crowd of profiteers and overturned their tables and benches. He also prevented people from misusing the temple courts as a shortcut to transport their merchandise (v. 16). It was high drama as Jesus cleaned out the temple with divine anger.

Then Jesus taught the crowd, some of whom may have looked on with amusement as He cleaned up the abuse and ungodly profiteering in the Court of the Gentiles. Jesus quoted Isaiah 56:7 and Jeremiah 7:11, repeating what God had said—His house would be "a house of prayer for all nations," meaning that Israel was supposed to lead the nations (Gentiles) to worship God. But the unfaithful people of God had turned the court into a "den of robbers" (Mark 11:17) instead. Seeing who they were up against, the chief priests and teachers of the law, who had profited from the ghastly commercialization of the temple, seriously plotted to kill Jesus (v. 18). They saw Him as a competition and threat.

Normally, leaves on a fig tree indicate that fruit is coming. On the way to the temple, Jesus cursed a fruitless tree that had fully leafed before the season for figs. It had given the false impression that it bore fruit when it actually did not. It represented what God's people had become—hypocritical and pretentious. The temple had its crowds but it was not bearing any spiritual fruit. The following day, the disciples saw the cursed tree "withered from the roots" (v. 20)—an object lesson of the consequences of stubborn disobedience and unfaithfulness, and a warning of impending judgment (the temple was destroyed by the Romans in AD 70). Then Jesus mentioned something about faith and fruitfulness. Faith in God can move mountains and is expressed in mountain-moving prayer (vv. 23–24). **Such faith also produces the power to forgive others even as we are forgiven by our Father (v. 25). Faith produces fruit.**

ThinkThrough

Are there examples today of how the church ignores its reason for existence and dabbles in commerce and other activities that distract it and destroy its mission? What will you do about it?

What sort of fruit is God looking for in us? How do we often sorely disappoint Him? Why is faith and obedience important in this?

Day 42

Read Mark 11:27–33

The religious leaders saw how Jesus had cleaned up the temple of its ungodly commercial business. They also saw how the "whole crowd was amazed at his teaching" (v. 18). Jesus acted with real authority, and according to Matthew 21:23 (cf. Luke 20:1), He also taught in the temple and the people loved it. The religious leaders tried to undermine Jesus's authority by questioning it. "By what authority are you doing these things . . . who gave you authority to do this?" (Mark 11:28). They were thinking "horizontally" instead of "vertically," looking to socially-derived authority instead of God's authority. They themselves drew authority from their pedigree (some were priests), rabbinic training, and recognition by religious authorities. So, who sent you? Where did you study theology? Who ordained you? These would have been the kinds of questions they had in mind. They knew that Jesus was a traveling preacher from simple, provincial Galilee. He did not seem to come from any established family or have formal theological training.

The religious leaders thought that by showing His poor curriculum vitae to the people they could get them to ignore this preacher from nowhere, and thus regain their authority. Jesus, of course, could have stated some amazing truths. He was the Son of God, sent by the Father (cf. John 8:12–19, 54–58). But He refused to answer their spurious questions. Instead He replied with a question. He asked them about John's baptism, whether it was from heaven or from men. **"Tell me!" He challenged them before the crowd (Mark 11:29–30). In doing so, He imposed His authority over them.** The tables had turned and now, in the presence of the Son of God, their authority was in question. All they could manage was, "We don't know" (v. 33).

It was not because they did not have an opinion. Actually, they did not think much of John the Baptist or anyone else outside of their special circle. They regarded themselves as exclusive spiritual leaders appointed by God, and were therefore unwilling to share their glory with others. They had discussed among themselves before answering Jesus. They knew that if they said that John's baptism was from heaven, then Jesus would question their disbelief of Him, for John had testified that Jesus was the Messiah. If they answered otherwise, the people would turn against them, for John had been very popular with the masses. So they gave a non-committal answer that aimed to save their skins. Their authority and concerns were only horizontal. Jesus therefore refused to answer them since they refused to answer His question (v. 33).

Consider how authority is derived in the church and how it is exercised. Why is authority derived from structures, skills, and popular acclaim potentially dangerous? How can true spiritual authority be recognized?

What can we learn from Jesus in handling troublemakers whose questions are not sincere or helpful to them or others?

Day 43

Read Mark 12:1–12

Though He refused to answer their question about His authority, Jesus did provide an answer that the religious leaders did not expect. He told a story. An owner of the land planted a vineyard and rented it to some farmers, and went away for quite a while. When harvest time came, he sent a servant to get his rightful share of the fruit, but his servant was beaten and sent away empty handed. Other servants who followed were treated just as badly, and some were even killed. Then the owner sent his own son, who he thought would be respected. But they killed him too. Jesus then said that the owner would return to destroy all those who killed his son.

It is clear what Jesus was referring to. The owner of the vineyard is God. We read in Isaiah 5:7 that "The vineyard of the LORD Almighty is the nation of Israel." God sent many prophets to the unfaithful nation, only to be rejected. Then He sent His only Son, Jesus, who would be killed by them.

Here then is the authority of Jesus. He is none other than the Son of God, and He has the authority of God Himself, far above any others. But the Jews rejected the authority of Jesus. Instead they were trying to kill Him. This would be held against them.

Jesus quoted Scripture ("The stone the builders rejected has become the cornerstone"; Psalm 118:22) to say that He would have the final word and determine the final outcome. This Palm Sunday psalm introduces the coming of the Messiah. How people respond to Him will determine their destiny. "Everyone who falls on that stone will be broken to pieces; anyone on whom it falls will be crushed" (Luke 20:18). **Jesus has the authority and power to both forgive (those whose hearts are broken by His message) and punish (those who reject Him).**

The religious leaders knew that Jesus was referring to them and dared not reply, because they could not. Their authority was man-made and feeble and they were afraid of the people (Mark 12:12). Their authority, it seems, was made or broken by the people, not God. They were more afraid of people than they were of God. How pathetic!

Why did Jesus answer the religious leaders with a parable? Why is it difficult to refute a parable? They "left him and went away" (v. 12). What should they have done? How do Christians walk away from a parable of Jesus?

What does the parable say about the authority of Jesus? How is His authority expressed in the disciple's life? Assess your own experience in the light of this.

Day 44

Read Mark 12:13–17

Jesus's enemies tried to entrap Him by asking many trick questions. Although He didn't have anyone to advise or help Him, Jesus handled the situation exceptionally well.

The religious leaders sent some Pharisees and Herodians "to catch him in his words" (v. 13). These two groups hated each other as they stood for diametrically opposed principles and values. One was culturally and religiously ultra-conservative and the other was liberal. Now that they had a common enemy, they joined forces against Jesus. They asked Him a question about whether Jews should pay a poll tax to the Roman emperor. Knowing that some Jews refused to pay the tax as it would be acknowledging their subjection to Rome, they attempted to force Jesus into a tight corner. Their "either-or" question was intended to land Jesus in trouble whichever way He answered—as a supporter of Rome or a rebel against it. They flattered Jesus by saying He was a "man of integrity" who was not "swayed by others" (v. 14).

Seeing through their hypocrisy, Jesus asked them why they were trying to trap Him (v. 15). Everyone knew that and waited to see how He would handle the situation. He asked for a denarius, a Roman coin, and asked whose portrait was on it. When they replied that it was Caesar's, He said, "Give back to Caesar what is Caesar's and to God what is God's" (v. 17). The crowd must have been elated, and may even have applauded, when they saw how well Jesus had defeated the trick question.

But there was a more important lesson. Just as the coin had Caesar's image on it, the human soul has God's image on it. **We were all created in the image of God (Genesis 1:26). Though this image has been marred, it still reminds us that we belong to God, not to ourselves or anyone else.** When we recognize this and give ourselves back to God, then His grace will work within us to re-establish His image in us through His Son (Romans 8:29; 1 Corinthians 15:49). Instead of talking politics, the questioners of Jesus should be thinking of the state of their souls and their relationship with God.

ThinkThrough

How would it feel to be continually under scrutiny by hostile people who want to harm you? Try to put yourself in Jesus's shoes, and thank Him for His faithfulness and wisdom—all for your sake.

What does Jesus teach about rising above temporal questions to probe more deeply into spiritual realities? People often ask questions that hide underlying spiritual need. How can you develop greater discernment in this?

Day 45

Read Mark 12:18–27

Unlike the Pharisees, the Sadducees did not believe in the resurrection. They considered only the first five books of the Old Testament (the Torah) as authoritative and claimed that they do not teach about a resurrection. Their trick question had to do with an Old Testament provision for Levirate marriage (Deuteronomy 25:5; cf. Ruth 3:9; 4:10). They gave a case study (probably cooked up) of a woman who had seven husbands who were brothers—one after another. The trick question: "At the resurrection, whose wife will she be?" (Mark 12:23). This was not an innocent question; it was set to trap Jesus (and perhaps also as a side dig at the Pharisees).

Jesus gave a fairly long answer. Firstly, he confirmed that there will be a resurrection and an afterlife ("When the dead rise"; v. 25). He used Scripture, from the Torah of Moses itself (Exodus 3:6), to explain this—using the term "the God of Abraham, the God of Isaac, and the God of Jacob" (Mark 12:26). God is present with all generations, even those from the past. He is the God of the living (v. 27). Secondly He showed that their idea of heaven was wrong. It will be a different order; there will be no marriage. People will be like the angels (v. 25), which the Sadducees didn't believe in (Acts 23:8). The only family in heaven will be the family of God where God is the Father and everyone will be His child. We will all be brothers and sisters in Christ. There would be no need for marriage as there would be no need to procreate as on earth (Genesis 1:28; 9:1).

The Lord's answer challenged the distorted beliefs and thinking of the Sadducees. This was sweet news to the shrewd Pharisees (teachers of the law) who responded "Well said, teacher!" (Luke 20:39). For a moment, they forgot their mission to entrap Jesus and commended Him. Why? They were opposed to the Sadducees on doctrinal issues (cf. Paul's use of this division for his own defense in Acts 23:6–10). But Jesus did not accept the compliment. He knew their wicked hearts.

Jesus faulted the Sadducees for their ignorance about two things: God's Word and God's power (Mark 12:24).

They knew neither God's truth nor His almighty power. Their rejection of the resurrection was an indication of their ignorance. They thought they had figured out everything in God's Word and understood all He could do, when in fact they knew nothing. How can they be trusted as leaders?

The Sadducees read only the Torah. Why is selective reading of Scripture dangerous? Resolve and study the whole of God's Word—all 66 books in the Bible.

Why does lack of knowledge of God's Word and God's power produce error? Can you think of some contemporary examples of people being "badly mistaken" (v. 27)? What steps can you take to know the Scriptures and God's power better?

Day 46

Read Mark 12:28–34

A teacher of the law—probably a Pharisee—was impressed with the way Jesus handled the Sadducees (v. 28). He then asked Jesus which among the 613 commandments that devout Jews observed was the most important.

Jesus readily answered him by quoting Deuteronomy 6:4–5 and Leviticus 19:18. We are to love God with all our heart, soul, mind, and strength (Mark 12:30). We are also to love our neighbor as ourselves (v. 31). Jesus summarized the two sections of the Ten Commandments, the first dealing with our vertical relationship with God, and the second dealing with our horizontal relationships with others. **By stating the commandments in this way, Jesus put the focus on right relationships marked by love. This was at the heart of biblical religion.** The ancient prophets of Israel had spoken against the two sins of the nation: idolatry and social injustice (Amos 2:4–8). These were results of disobeying the commandments of God.

When Jesus becomes our Lord and Savior, we are given power to turn from idols and "serve the living and true God" (1 Thessalonians 1:9). This is what the risen Jesus told Peter when He reinstated him into ministry. Peter was to love Jesus and to love His sheep by feeding them faithfully (John 21:15–17). True religion is seeking holiness and caring for the needy (James 1:27); the motives are love for God and others.

The law teacher commended Jesus for His answer and agreed with Him (Mark 12:32–33). He honored Jesus with the title "Teacher" (v. 32). He also emphasized what Scripture taught— that to love God and others is more important than "all burnt offerings and sacrifices" (v. 33; cf. 1 Samuel 15:22; Hosea 6:6; Micah 6:6–8). Jesus was pleased with the man's responses, for he had "answered wisely," and told him, "You are not far from the kingdom of God" (v. 34). The man had the right understanding of Scripture and what God required of His people. He also had the right attitude towards Jesus. If he went further and expressed faith in Jesus as the promised Messiah, he would enter the kingdom. He was that close to it—personal faith in Jesus was all that remained.

ThinkThrough

Why do you think love is at the heart of God's commandments? What does it say about ritualistic and moralistic religion that is motivated by attitudes other than love? Consider your own love for God and others in this light.

Think of people you know who may not be far from the kingdom of God. What keeps them from taking the decisive step into the kingdom? Pray for them by name.

Day 47

Read Mark 12:35–40

All Jesus's opponents fell silent when they realized they were no match for Him. The last man to ask Jesus a question had in fact asked with sincerity, on the very verge of believing.

As there were no more questions from them, Jesus Himself asked one (vv. 35–37). The teachers of the law taught that the Messiah (Christ) was the son (descendant) of David. Jesus, quoting from Psalm 110:1, then pointed out that David, inspired by the Holy Spirit, had addressed the Messiah as "Lord" (Mark 12:37). How could the Messiah be merely David's earthly descendant if David paid homage to Him (Peter later used this verse in his Pentecost sermon to demonstrate the divinity of Jesus)?

As Matthew 22:46 records, there was an embarrassing silence as the religious leaders who had come to trap Jesus with their clever questions hung their heads in shame, unable to give a proper answer. They must have wondered, "Where does this simple Galilean learn to speak so well? Does he have a secret teacher?" Each silent minute made them look more and more ignorant. The large crowd watched all this with elation (Mark 12:37). Never had they seen their pompous leaders silenced in this way. These religious leaders failed to see that Jesus was both "the Root and the Offspring of David"—that the Messiah was not merely a descendant, but also the divine Lord and Creator of David (Revelation 22:16).

Jesus then openly criticized His critics and warned the people, "Watch out for the teachers of the law" (Mark 12:38). They were self-centered men who sought worldly honor. They liked to "walk around in flowing robes and be greeted with respect in the marketplaces." The religious leaders clenched their fists in anger as the crowd chuckled with delight—Jesus had described them so accurately and publicly ridiculed their hollow religion of appearances. They made lengthy prayers to impress others (v. 40), but God was not moved by them. They claimed all the best seats of honor (v. 39). But their actions were even more sinister and evil. They devoured widows' houses, cheating them of their only property and means of survival (v. 40).

Jesus condemned the religious leaders' hypocrisy and evil. In describing their behavior and motives, Jesus demonstrated that God had been watching them closely and would punish them severely (v. 40). Anyone who believed and followed them would suffer the same consequences.

Compare and consider the responses to the identity of Jesus as portrayed in Psalm 110:1: the religious leaders, the crowd, and the people at Pentecost listening to Peter in Acts 2. What do their various responses tell you?

Consider Jesus's strong criticism of the teachers of the law. How did He expose them and why do you think He had such harsh words for them? What would Jesus say today if He visited our churches?

Day 48

Read Mark 12:41–44

After a tiring time dealing with His opponents, Jesus sat down in the temple. But notice where He sat—in front of the offering box! (v. 41). Imagine Jesus doing this in church today.

There were 13 trumpet-shaped metal receptacles (*Shopharoth*) present for people to deposit their temple offerings. Coins tossed inside (there was no paper money yet) would make quite a bit of noise, attracting attention, especially if a rich man unloaded a large bag of them—a few at a time—just to impress others. The Greek text indicates that Jesus closely observed what was going on. There are "many rich people [who] threw in large amounts" (v. 41).

But Jesus drew attention to a poor widow who "put in two very small copper coins" (v. 42). This was a meager sum. Naturally no one had taken any notice of her, except Jesus, who was impressed. He declared that the widow had given more than all the rest, more than all of their gifts combined! Imagine a huge pile of offerings holding down one end of a balance scale, only to be outweighed by two tiny coins! This suggests that heaven keeps its ledgers differently from the world. As William Hendriksen

puts it, in Jesus's estimate, "the two copper coins were sparkling diamonds".[9]

This widow was possibly one of those who had been "devoured" by the hypocritical and evil teachers of the law (v. 40). Widows at this time were nobodies and had no social security. This woman probably had to beg on the street for the coins. She could have kept at least one of the coins for herself, it would not have made any real difference, but she didn't. Instead, she had given both to God.

This woman's gift became the best-known offering to God in church history! An insignificant amount in the eyes of the world, and yet in God's sight a most remarkable gift. She had given "everything—all she had to live on" (v. 44). **With no resources, she flung herself on God's mercy. She gave to express her faith in God, love for Him, and commitment to Him.** She would rather offer herself to God and die, than cling on to a couple of coins and try to survive on her own.

[9] William Hendriksen, *New Testament Commentary: Mark* (Edinburg: Banner of Truth Trust, 1975).

Why is how we give as important, if not more important than what we give? What is the difference between giving out of wealth and giving out of poverty? How can you apply this truth in your own life?

Why is Jesus so interested in our giving? What does this reveal about our hearts and quality of discipleship? What is the connection between giving and faith, and love and commitment? Pray about applying these lessons in your own life.

Day 49

Read Mark 13:1–25

Like gawking tourists, the disciples were very impressed by the size and beauty of the temple in Jerusalem (v. 1). But Jesus told them that it would all be reduced to rubble one day (v. 2). This was fulfilled in AD 70, when the Romans destroyed the city and its temple after a major Jewish revolt. The disciples questioned Jesus about the future and, in what became known as the Olivet Discourse (because Jesus delivered it on the Mount of Olives, v. 3), He painted a picture of events that would follow, until His glorious return. Peter, James, and John (the inner circle of disciples) were joined by Andrew, and they privately asked Jesus two questions: When would these things happen? What would be the signs that they are happening (v. 4)?

Jesus painted a disturbing picture, spelling out some of the signs that would mark "the beginning of birth pains" (v. 8). Just as a woman felt distressing labor pangs announcing the impending delivery of her child, so too would there be signs that the end was approaching. There would be false Christs (v. 6), wars (v. 7), earthquakes, and famines (v. 8), and believers would face tribulation and persecution (v. 9). God would enable His people to preach the gospel to all nations (v. 10). He would not abandon them, and "he who stands firm to the end will be saved" (v. 13).

Worse things would happen. The "abomination that causes desolation" referred to historical anti-Christs such as Antiochus IV Epiphanes, a Greek ruler who killed thousands of Jews and desecrated the Jerusalem Temple in 167 BC by sacrificing pigs on its altar and installing a heathen idol in its sanctuary (v. 14; cf. Daniel 9:27; 11:31; 12:11). There would also be future anti-Christs who would bring unimaginable desecration and suffering (Mark 13:14–20)—only the mercy of God would prevent total annihilation. False Christs and prophets would continue to plague the world and the church and "perform signs and wonders" (vv. 21–23). The followers of Christ ("the elect") were warned against being taken in.

Then strange cosmic disturbances would take place. Jesus pointed the disciples to the prophecies in Isaiah 13:10 and 34:4, where the skies would become the scene of alarming sights: sun and moon both darkening, stars falling from the sky, and other heavenly bodies shaking (vv. 24–25). The history of the world would hurtle towards a terrifying end, with trouble on earth and turmoil in the skies. But **Christians should take heart that God would be in control. Christ would return to establish His rule and order.**

The Jews thought highly of the magnificent-looking temple, but Jesus is greater than the temple (Matthew 12:6). How important is it to keep our eyes on Jesus rather than on anything else (cf. 2 Corinthians 4:18), no matter how impressive?

What abiding practical lessons are there in Mark 13? Turn your thoughts into prayer.

Read Mark 13:26–31

After these distressing days, when there would be chaos on earth and in the skies, Jesus, the Son of Man, would return "in clouds with great power and glory" (v. 26). He would gather His elect from everywhere and establish His kingdom forever (v. 27). This general outline of the future is followed by John in Revelation. We read in Revelation 1:7 that Jesus would return in the clouds and that everyone would see Him. He would judge the living and the dead and establish His kingdom forever. Jesus would exercise His divine authority, for only God has the authority to dispatch angels to do His bidding and to be the ultimate Judge.

Like many Old Testament prophecies, the events Jesus foretells span a broad sweep of time, from the near to the distant future. His words are a theological telescope that shows both what would happen soon after the Olivet discourse—the destruction of Jerusalem in AD 70—and the distant future at the end of history, when Jesus shall return.

When Jesus told the parable of the fig tree, the lesson was applicable to both the terrible destruction of Jerusalem at the hands of the Roman army, less than four decades away, and to the devastation of the end times. This is in keeping with many biblical prophecies which can be applied to both the intermediate as well as the distant future. There were many fig trees in Israel and everyone knew that when the trees began to sprout leaves, it was a sign that summer was nearing. It also meant that harvest time would follow. Therefore, when the signs mentioned by Jesus occurred, people were to expect that "it is near, right at the door" (Mark 13:29). The "it" referred to the end when Jesus would return.

There was one puzzling statement of Jesus (v. 30). Why did He say that these things will be fulfilled during the lifetime of His listeners? Actually, they were partially fulfilled in AD 70 when Jerusalem fell to the Roman army. The Jewish historian Flavius Josephus records the details of this tragic event. The city suffered a terrible siege and was finally destroyed, along with its temple. More than a million people were said to have been killed. The "abomination that causes desolation" (v. 14) is seen by some scholars as referring to the Roman soldiers planting their standards and worshiping their gods in the ruins of the temple during the fall of the city. It is in this regard that the phrase "this generation" (v. 30) may have meant "this race of Jews."

Jesus's prophecy, fulfilled partially in AD 70, awaits total fulfillment in the future.

In the light of what Jesus taught in Mark 13, why do you think He wept over Jerusalem in Luke 19:41–44? What does it say about how we should pray for our world in which the majority do not recognize the coming of God?

What personal implication is there for you that the elect would be gathered from everywhere (v. 27)? How would you pray for yourself and for others?

Day 51

Read Mark 13:32–37

The disciples asked Jesus two questions. He answered their second question at length, describing the signs that would precede the destruction of the temple in Jerusalem (v. 2). This destruction would take place in AD 70. While answering the disciples' question Jesus also described more distant events in the future, prior to His return. There would be great social, spiritual, and natural disturbances and instability. The entire description was unsettling and deeply disturbing.

But Jesus did not answer the disciples' first question about timing—when everything would happen. Instead He stated that only the Father knew when the end will take place. The angels did not know, and neither did the Son of God (v. 32). **His purpose for putting it this way was to warn everyone to "Be on guard! Be alert!" (v .33). There was no place for spiritual complacency.**

Jesus told another parable to help them understand. The owner of a house went away but did not say when he would be back. He left his servants with various responsibilities, "each with his assigned task" (v. 34). One servant was placed at the door; his specific task was to look out for his master's return, a task he would not be able to perform if he fell asleep and stopped keeping watch. Jesus warned everyone that He would return again to earth suddenly, and the only way people could be prepared for His coming as Judge and King (see Matthew 25:13) was to stay spiritually awake and alert (Mark 13:35–37).

While some today try to predict where we are in the prophetic program for the future, trying to connect the prophecies of Jesus with current events, many others do not bother with Jesus's warning. For both these groups, Jesus had something to say: don't be presumptuous; nobody knows, except the Father, when the final end will come (vv. 32–34). It may come suddenly (vv. 35–37). The best thing to do is to remain vigilant and "keep watch" (v. 34; cf. vv. 5, 9).

We can be sure that everything will happen just as Jesus prophesied. "Heaven and earth will pass away, but my words will never pass away" (v. 31). The words of Jesus must be taken seriously, in faith and obedience.

What do you think would happen if the exact date of the return of Jesus is known? How would it affect the quality of discipleship among Christians?

Many Christians do not take seriously the truth that Jesus will return suddenly and unexpect- edly. What does His command to "keep watch" mean for you personally? What "assigned task" (Mark 13:34) do you have?

Day 52

Read Mark 14:1–11

Dark clouds were gathering around Jesus. The religious leaders were seriously plotting to kill Him (vv. 1–2). He was about to be sacrificed like a Passover lamb for the sin of the whole world (John 1:29). Even His disciples failed to appreciate what is about to happen. But Jesus drew comfort from Mary of Bethany, who was always to be found at the feet of Jesus, listening attentively to Him (Luke 10:39; John 11:32). John 12:1–8 records the same event.

Jesus was having a meal when Mary brought in a jar of "very expensive" perfume (v. 3) and shocked everyone by breaking it and pouring all its contents on Jesus's head (John focuses on Jesus's feet). She could have poured just a drop or two, but she worshiped Jesus generously. Mary was harshly rebuked for "wasting" such expensive perfume, which could have been sold to help the poor instead. How financially efficient these people were! Chief among the critics was Judas Iscariot (John 12:4–5), who as treasurer and thief could have helped himself to the money from the sale (12:6).

Jesus rebuked Judas and the other critics. He told them to leave Mary alone and commended her for having done a "beautiful thing to me" (Mark 14:6). She had prepared Him for burial (v. 8). **Having spent time at Jesus's feet actually listening to Him, she was likely the only one in the group who really understood what was about to happen to Jesus.** For her magnificent act of worship she would be remembered everywhere and for all time (v. 9).

At this point Judas turned decidedly against his Master. He took the traitorous steps of finding the chief priests and betraying Jesus. Why did he do it? Was he angry that Jesus rebuked him? Was he trying to force Jesus to accept His role as the political Messiah? Or was he just greedy? Matthew tells us that he tried bargaining with the chief priests but could only extract a meager sum for betraying Jesus (Matthew 26:15). The chief priests were delighted that they had found a treacherous ally among Jesus's disciples (v. 11). From the moment he criticized Mary for her beautiful act of devotion, Judas was on a dangerous downward slide to perdition. The man who accused Mary of wasting money would end up wasting (John 17:12, "lost" comes from the same Greek word) his whole life.

Mary knew more about Jesus and what was about to happen to Him than the Twelve. Why is it true that the Lord "confides in those who fear him" (Psalm 25:14; John 15:15)? Reflect on how you are spending time listening to Jesus.

Contrast the beautiful act of Mary with the treacherous act of Judas. Where did Judas go wrong? How can one avoid becoming like Judas?

Day 53

Read Mark 14:12–26

Jesus was crucified on the day after Passover, sacrificing Himself as the Passover Lamb to save the world (1 Corinthians 5:7). This meal that Jesus had with His disciples was richly woven around the Passover Feast of the Jews, and was one that Jesus had "eagerly desired" (Luke 22:15; the Greek word expresses very strong desire) to eat with His disciples. Hence the arrangements for it had an air of secrecy, lest Judas act prematurely and prevent the meal from taking place. Jesus sent His trusted disciples Peter and John (Luke 22:8) to make preparations. That prior arrangements had probably been made was indicated by the unusual sight of a man carrying a water jar (normally a task for women, Mark 14:13), who showed them the large upper room reserved for the meal (v. 15). Today we continue to celebrate this meal as the Lord's Supper, remembering our Lord's sacrifice for us with deep gratitude.

At the meal, Jesus told the disciples that one of them would betray Him (v. 18). It was most treacherous to betray a friend after having a meal with him. Dismayed, each disciple asked Jesus, "Surely you don't mean me?" (v. 19).

We too must look inward to examine ourselves. Jesus referred to Judas without naming him, offering him a chance to repent. Jesus would be crucified to fulfill God's plan, but Judas was responsible for his own terrible sin (v. 21).

Jesus then took, blessed, broke, and gave out the bread, and also the cup (vv. 22–23). He referred to them as "my body" and "my blood." They underline for us His sacrifice on the cross, and when we receive and eat and drink, we are expressing our trust in Him (1 Corinthians 11:26) and are sustained by His life in us (John 6:56). **Like Jesus, we must also look up with faith and trust (Psalm 123:1), and like the disciples, we look around with brotherly love as we eat the meal as the body of Christ (1 Corinthians 11:29).**

Jesus then pointed to the future when He would drink with His disciples again (Mark 14:25)—at the great wedding feast of the Lamb when He returns (Revelation 19:9). At the Lord's Table, we also look forward to this day with faith-filled anticipation.

Why has the church
continuously
celebrated the Lord's
Supper? What is its
significance and
how should it be
carried out?

Jesus "eagerly
desired" to have
the meal with His
disciples. Consider
how He wants to do
the same with you
(cf. Revelation 3:20).
How would you
respond to Him?

Day 54

Read Mark 14:27–31

Jesus looked sadly at His disciples, knowing that they would be scattered like frightened sheep. Quoting Zechariah 13:7, He told them "You will all fall away" (v. 27). But He gave them hope, saying that He would rise from the dead, and would meet them in Galilee later. As usual, without pausing to think deeply about what Jesus had said, Simon Peter boldly declared, "Even if all fall away, I will not" (v. 29). Full of self-confidence, Peter thought that his commitment to Jesus was especially strong. What he said must have offended the others—not to be outdone, all promptly made the same declaration (v. 31).

Jesus must have looked lovingly at Peter; though impulsive, he was also guileless. He meant well but often spoke wrongly and acted clumsily. Jesus said, "Simon, Simon, Satan has asked to sift all of you as wheat. But I have prayed for you, Simon, that your faith may not fail. And when you have turned back, strengthen your brothers" (Luke 22:31–32). Jesus revealed what will happen to Peter, who was ignorant of his true condition and the nature of the spiritual battle he was fighting. That very night, before the rooster crowed twice, Peter will disown his Lord three times (Mark 14:30; cf. 1 Corinthians 10:12).

Peter did not believe it. He was too sure of his strength under pressure. He "insisted emphatically" that he would stand by Jesus (v. 31). "Even if I have to die with you, I will never disown you." **It was nice to hear him speak like this, but Jesus knew his weaknesses, and looked at him with understanding eyes.** He knew that Peter would repent after denying Jesus, and the Lord would restore him and give him the responsibility of leading the disciples (cf. John 21). Jesus would also tell Peter later of how he must die for Him (John 21:18–19), Christian tradition tells how Peter was finally crucified in Rome for preaching the gospel.

After hearing Peter profess his undying love for Jesus, the other disciples also joined the chorus of voices asserting unshakeable commitment. Many of the songs we sing in church make bold assertions about how much we love the Lord and how we are willing to give up all to follow Him. We must take care that our bold pronouncements are more than the mere movement of our lips.

Why is it important not to think too highly of oneself but to act with sober judgment (Romans 12:3)? Jesus knows us better than we know ourselves. What is He saying to you? Have you said things to Him that you failed to carry out?

We are to humbly consider others better than ourselves (Philippians 2:3). Such humility must be learned from Jesus (2:5–11). How can one be humble and yet "obedient to death"?

Day 55

Read Mark 14:32–42

Gethsemane means "olive press," a place where olives were crushed for their oil. It was an appropriate name for the place where Jesus suffered intense agony as He prepared Himself for the cross. A man on death row would have all kinds of thoughts running through his mind, including the agony of death and the end of his earthly journey. Crucifixion was a cruel Roman punishment, intended to strike great fear in people. Its barbarity was unimaginable. Jesus would have to go through it, but it was not just the physical violence and the public humiliation of the cross that troubled Him.

His soul was "overwhelmed with sorrow to the point of death" (v. 34) because of the unparalleled suffering of carrying the world's sin on the cross (2 Corinthians 5:21). Who else could have understood such a crushing experience? Moreover, Jesus would have to face divine wrath and worse, the full consequences of the world's sins. It was the unimaginable spiritual suffering of the cross that overwhelmed Him (v. 34; cf. Hebrews 5:7–8).

Three times, Jesus implored His Father to take the cup (cf. Isaiah 51:17; Jeremiah 25:15) from Him. But He knew there was no other way to save the world of sinners except through the cross. So three times He submitted himself to the Father's will. All His life, He had sought to do the Father's will (John 6:38; 8:28–29; Hebrews 10:7) and now He was truly "obedient to death" (Philippians 2:8). **How much more should we give up our self-will and submit to God's will! In self-denial, we must carry the cross to follow Jesus (Luke 9:23). There is no other way.**

The three disciples—Peter, James, and John—who were asked to pray with Jesus in Gethsemane failed to provide human company and comfort, letting Him down. Though He asked them to stay there and keep watch (Mark 14:34), they fell asleep. Three times He found them sleeping. Jesus had just told Peter that he and the others would be sorely tested, yet they slept through it all. Prayerlessness is a sure recipe for falling into temptation (v. 38). "The spirit is willing, but the flesh is weak" (v. 38). What a contrast: Jesus falling to the ground in agonizing prayer, and the disciples, curled up on the ground in comfortable sleep! Who will pray with Jesus?

Why was Jesus deeply distressed in Gethsemane? How would His relationship with His Father be affected when He later had to carry the sins of the world on the cross? Take time to thank Jesus for what He went through in Gethsemane and on the cross for you.

Christians often do not have deep struggles between pursuing their will and embracing God's will. If this is true, why so? Is there any area in your life where you have to clearly abandon your will to pursue God's will? Turn your thoughts into prayer.

Read Mark 14:43–52

t was time for the sheep to be scattered. The betrayer Judas arrived with a crowd of armed men. As prearranged, he betrayed Jesus with the treacherous kiss of a false friend (vv. 44–45). The armed men "seized Jesus and arrested him" (v. 46). Imagine the scene. How would Jesus respond?

Peter drew his sword and sliced off the ear of the high priest's servant (v. 47; John 18:10). John records the victim's name—Malchus. This being both a traumatic and transforming incident for him, Malchus could have been converted later and joined the church, and this may be the reason why his name is mentioned. Peter, the impulsive fisherman, had become a swordsman. To his credit, he had acted courageously, living up to his recent boast. He may still have harbored the idea that Jesus would turn the tables and establish His strong political kingdom. Surely swords would be necessary. The Lord who multiplied two fish could surely multiply the swords to gain an astounding victory! Earlier, when Jesus asked the disciples to sell their cloaks to buy swords, they misunderstood and told Him they already had two swords. And He said, "That's enough" (Luke 22:36–38). It is easy to see how Peter could have misunderstood Jesus and thought of using his sword to defend Him. The battle for the kingdom had begun. But one sword was hardly a match for an army of swords! However, there was another sword—not physical but spiritual—that was up to the task: the sword of the Spirit (Ephesians 6:17), which Peter later found had the power to cut open stubborn and sinful hearts (Acts 2:37).

Although not recorded in Mark's gospel, Luke 22:51 tells us that Jesus then healed the high priest's servant's ear. It was an act of compassion and a rejection of any idea that Jesus was leading an armed rebellion (Mark 14:48). **Jesus made it clear that the Scriptures must be fulfilled (v. 49; cf. Isaiah 53:7–12) and that He was prepared to go to the cross.** Then "everyone deserted him and fled" (v. 50). Peter had the courage to carry a sword but not a cross.

The young man who "fled naked" (vv. 51–52), mentioned only in Mark, is believed to be Mark himself, who humbly notes that he too lost courage and joined the fleeing disciples.

Why do you think the disciples may have misunderstood about the swords? How can we misunderstand Jesus and employ means to further His kingdom that are foreign to His ways?

Is it easier to carry a sword or a cross? Reflect on this in terms of your various situations—at home, at the workplace, in church, in your neighborhood, and in the world.

Read Mark 14:53–72

The arrest of Jesus was followed by a kangaroo court convened at night. He was tried by the highest Jewish council and court, the Sanhedrin, comprising the chief priests, elders, and teachers of the law, and presided over by the high priest. They tried to find evidence that would condemn Jesus to capital punishment (vv. 55–59) but had a tough time doing so, because Jesus was innocent. He remained silent (v. 61). Then they asked Jesus whether He was the Messiah and Son of God, and Jesus replies He was (v. 62). They now had a charge—blasphemy—and sentenced Him to death (v. 64). **Jesus was then spat upon, mocked, and beaten (v. 65). Justice went to sleep that night.**

Peter had followed the arrested Jesus "at a distance" (v. 54). While Jesus suffered at the hands of the corrupt Sanhedrin, Peter found some comfort outside warming himself at a fire (v. 54). A servant girl of the high priest passed by and recognised him as a disciple of Jesus (v. 67). Peter had been crouching in the darkness in relative safety, but was now exposed by a servant girl.

Peter tried to save his own skin by denying that he was a disciple of Jesus and by changing location (v. 68). He lied by claiming that he didn't know or understand what the girl was talking about. One reason people lie is to get out of trouble. The servant girl was quite sure that Peter was one of the disciples and she told others standing around, "This fellow is one of them" (v. 69). Now quite upset with her (these high priest's servants were such a nuisance), Peter again had to deny that he was Jesus's disciple (v. 70).

People began to notice Peter. Perhaps it was his Galilean accent, or his furtive glances and guilty, anxious look. They then said, "Surely you are one of them, for you are a Galilean" (v. 70). This time Peter reacted more strongly, swearing and vehemently denying that he knew "this man" (v. 71). Just then, the rooster crowed for the second time, just as Jesus had predicted (v. 72; Mark 14:30). Luke describes it as an intensely personal experience, for at that point Jesus "turned and looked straight at Peter" (Luke 22:61). That look spoke a thousand words. Peter was convicted, and he "broke down and wept" in bitterness and shame (Mark 14:72).

Why did Jesus for the most part remain silent at the Sanhedrin? Why did He allow sinful and wicked men to try Him at court? How could they be allowed to condemn God for blasphemy? Think of how Jesus would personally answer you. Turn your thoughts into prayer.

Was there a connection between Peter's prayerlessness (vv. 37–38), and his fall? How do Christians end up denying Jesus? Why does this happen? Pray for yourself.

Read Mark 15:1–15

The religious leaders brought Jesus first thing in the morning to the Roman governor Pontius Pilate, who was a cruel man. They needed to do this because the Roman government had in AD 7 taken away the Jews' right to put their criminals to death (John 18:31). They resented this, but often exercised it when the authorities looked the other way (e.g. Stephen's martyrdom, Acts 7). To put Jesus to death on their own would have been too dangerous for them, for He was a well-known figure. So they brought Him to Pilate. If the charge was that He thought of Himself as God, Pilate would have merely laughed, for the Romans had hundreds of gods. So instead they charged Jesus with a political crime; that He claimed to be the king of the Jews. This would be considered seditious by the Romans.

But Pilate disliked the Jews. Following legal procedure, he asked Jesus about being the king of the Jews, to which Jesus replied, "You have said so" (Mark 15:2). Pilate must have responded with an understanding smile. So the religious leaders poured on more accusations (v. 3). But Jesus remained silent and Pilate was "amazed" to see that He did not defend Himself (v. 5). Pilate knew that Jesus was innocent (Luke 23:14), the victim of the envious religious leaders (Mark 15:10), and tried to find reasons to release Him without causing a riot. It was customary for a prisoner, named by the people, to be released during the Feast. Pilate asked whether they wanted Jesus released (v. 9). But the chief priests stirred up the crowd to ask for another prisoner, Barabbas, to be released instead (v. 11). This man was a rebel and murderer (v. 7).

Pilate then asked the crowd what was to be done about Jesus (v. 12). The judge asked the mob to sentence Jesus! They wanted Him crucified, and kept shouting even when Pilate asked them why Jesus deserved death (v. 14). Pilate was a coward, more afraid of public opinion than his own conscience. "Wanting to satisfy the crowd" he handed Jesus over to be crucified (v. 15). **Barabbas means "son of a father." The people had rejected the true "Son of the Father" for a man whose name represented all of us. Truly, Jesus died on the cross in place of the Barabbas in each of us.**

ThinkThrough

Reflect on the various characters in the text: the religious leaders, Pilate, the crowd. Compare them with Jesus, who was the only calm person in the scene, though He was the one who suffered. If you were present, what would you have done?

Barabbas was released and Jesus was crucified. Jesus hung on the sinner's cross and was pierced by the nails meant for Barabbas. Consider yourself released from the prison of sin because Jesus took your place. Say a prayer of thanksgiving to Jesus.

Read Mark 15:16–32

The Lord received very different treatment compared to a few days earlier when He rode into the city (Mark 11:7–10). This time, hardened soldiers flogged Him (15:15), an unimaginably painful punishment that tore flesh and left the victim near death. Then they made fun of Him since He had acknowledged being the king of the Jews (vv. 17–18). Soon after His birth, He had been worshiped as king by some Magi (Matthew 2:2, 11), but now rough military hands used to killing forced a purple robe (a royal color) on His torn back and a crown of thorns on His head (v. 17). They hit Him repeatedly on His head and spat on Him, and mockingly paid homage to Him on their knees (v. 19). He was a bloody sight. Then they took off the purple robe, tearing it from His bleeding back.

They led Him to be crucified outside the city on a small hill called Golgotha (v. 22). On the way, they conscripted Simon from Cyrene and father of Rufus (v. 21; possibly the same Rufus in Romans 16:13) to carry the cross for Jesus, severely weakened from the brutal torture. They offered Jesus a wine mixture to dull His pain and senses, but He refused it (v. 23). After crucifying Him at the third hour (9 a.m.), they cast lots for His clothes (v. 24; foretold in Psalm 22:18, which also meant that they stripped Him naked to suffer public humiliation). They wrote His charge and hung the notice on the cross: "The King of the Jews." This notice carried more meaning than they had intended. Two thieves were also crucified by His sides (v. 27; Isaiah 53:12). He became the object of ridicule from both passersby and the religious leaders (vv. 29–31; cf. Psalm 22:7). They challenged Him to come down from the cross in order to save Himself and prove who He claimed to be. But Jesus kept Himself fixed to the cross to save them and all of us, perhaps discerning Satan's tempting whispers behind all the noisy taunts. He could have come down with overpowering heavenly power, but that would have been the end of us all, for we would then be without the Savior, bound for hell. **In addition to physical agony, Jesus had to suffer the insults of the beneficiaries of His death.** Even the crucified thieves insulted Him (v. 32; though one later repented, see Luke 23:40–43).

ThinkThrough

In the light of the large number of prophecies detailing the crucifixion and sufferings of Jesus, how would the suffering Savior be comforted? How does this reassure you about who He is?

Jesus held back His power for our sake and accepted extreme violence, public humiliation, and unbearable insults. Take time to thank Him for His profound love for you and all of us.

Day 60

Read Mark 15:33–47

The land was filled with darkness from noon to 3 p.m. (v. 33). It was as if heaven dimmed the lights at the appalling sight of the Almighty Creator being killed by His sinful creatures (cf. Amos 8:9). Bearing the full weight of our sins, Jesus cried out loudly in Aramaic, "My God, my God, why have you forsaken me" (v. 34; Psalm 22:1). He who always addressed His Father as "Abba" was now forced to stand on the side of sinful humanity and face the full consequences of sin—separation from God. Someone tried to offer him wine vinegar to dull His pain and quench His thirst (v. 36; Psalm 69:21). Then with a loud cry, Jesus died.

At that moment, the curtain in the temple that covered the Most Holy Place was "torn in two from top to bottom" (v. 38), thus creating new access to the holy God (Hebrews 10:19–20). Before this, only the high priest was allowed to go beyond the curtain, once every year. The priests who were ministering in the temple must have seen this unbelievable event; perhaps the reason why some time later, "a large number of priests became obedient to the faith" (Acts 6:7). The Roman centurion who saw Jesus die was impressed: "Surely this man was the Son of God" (Mark 15:39).

Though all the male disciples (except John, see John 19:26) had run away, many women who followed Jesus were present. Among them were Mary Magdalene, another Mary, and Salome (v. 40). Without swords and totally helpless, these women could only offer Jesus their teary presence—and they did with courage and love.

As Sabbath was fast approaching, the burial must be done before sunset. There was a man called Joseph of Arimathea who was a member of the Sanhedrin and a secret believer (v. 43; John 19:38); he had disagreed with his murderous colleagues when they sentenced Jesus to death (Luke 23:51). He now went boldly to Pilate and asked for permission to bury Jesus. Together with Nicodemus, a Pharisee and most likely also a believer (John 3:1–8; 19:39–40), Joseph placed the body in a new tomb that belonged to him. This fulfilled the prophecy in Isaiah 53:9, for Joseph was a rich man (see Matthew 27:57). A stone was rolled to block the entrance. And the two Marys noted where the tomb was. But why does Mark provide all these details? To prepare us for the events that followed.

Why was the curtain in the temple torn from top to bottom (v. 38)? What do you think was God's message? We have gained access to God through Jesus (Romans 5:2). Speak to Jesus with gratitude and assess how you are making use of this privilege bought with His blood.

What can we learn from the women and Joseph, who courageously asked to bury Jesus? How did they show their love for Jesus? How can you apply these lessons in your life?

Day 61

Read Mark 16:1–8

On Saturday evening, when the Sabbath was over, the two Marys and Salome who were present at the cross (Mark 15:40) brought spices to anoint the body of Jesus (16:1). Early the next morning, they went to the tomb, and it dawned on them that they might not be able to move the stone at the entrance, which could be closed with relative ease by slotting it into a groove on the rock floor, but was very difficult to open afterwards (v. 3). Perhaps they should have brought some of the male disciples to help them.

They got a shock when they reached the tomb: the entrance stone had already been moved (v. 4). That it was not the wrong tomb is made clear by Mark 15:47—they knew where it was. Rushing in, they were further shocked to see someone sitting inside it. It was a young man dressed in a white robe (an angel, according to Matthew 28:5). He told them not to be alarmed, and that Jesus had risen (Mark 16:6)! He showed them the place where Jesus's body had been—it was empty. He then instructed the astounded women to tell the disciples of Jesus, "and Peter" (a special touch of the forgiving Lord who felt for the fumbling and repentant Peter), that Jesus had risen and was going ahead of them into Galilee, where they would see Him again (v. 7). Jesus had already told them about this (Mark 14:28).

That God chose women to be the first witnesses of the resurrection is incredible, if we remember that in the culture of those days, the testimony of women was not taken seriously (vv. 9–11; Luke 24:10–11). **If the resurrection of Jesus was invented, the "inventors" would have placed men as the first witnesses.** That the women were the first to see the empty tomb and meet the angel is surely proof of the authenticity of the resurrection account.

The women were "trembling" (the Greek word means "ecstasy"), "bewildered," and "afraid" (v. 8). They ran away from the tomb, after the shock of seeing it empty and being told that Jesus had risen. They were afraid yet filled with joy.

Put yourself in the women's sandals. How would you have reacted to what they saw and heard? Why did the disciples and women find it hard to believe what Jesus has already predicted (Mark 8:31; 9:31; 10:34)?

What does the resurrection of Jesus prove about who Jesus is? Remember that Mark 1:1 refers to Jesus as "the Son of God." Remembering that you are also a witness of the risen Lord, how would that change your life?

Day 62

Read Mark 16:9–20

There is considerable doubt among scholars about whether verses 9–20 belong to the original text of Mark, as the earliest manuscripts do not include them. If so, Mark seems to end abruptly. Was it because he was killed before he could conclude his gospel, or was his conclusion simply lost? Attempts seem to have been made to give the book a proper ending through later additions. A short conclusion is added in some manuscripts stating that Jesus sent His disciples east and west with the gospel. In other manuscripts this passage (vv. 9–20) is included. These endings are recognized as not present in the original text. Nevertheless, this passage is included in most Bibles.

We have the unusual note that Jesus rebuked the disciples for "their lack of faith" and "stubborn refusal to believe" the witnesses He had sent (v. 14). Why so? In Scripture, matters were to be established with two or three witnesses (Deuteronomy 19:15; cf. Matthew 18:16; 2 Corinthians 13:1). Jesus had sent three witnesses to the disciples: Mary Magdalene (Mark 16:9) and two others who were "walking in the country" (v. 12, these were the two who were walking on the road to Emmaus; Luke 24:13–35).

When Mary told the disciples what she had seen, "they did not believe it" (Mark 16:11). When the two men also told the disciples what they had witnessed, "they did not believe them either" (v. 13). Hence, Jesus rebuked the skeptical disciples.

Jesus then told the disciples (and continues to tell us all) to "Go into all the world and preach the gospel to all creation," assuring them that anyone who "believes and is baptized will be saved" but anyone who "does not believe will be condemned" (vv. 15–16). Jesus promised to give them some amazing signs: the power to drive out demons, to speak in new tongues, to pick up snakes and drink poison without being harmed, and to heal the sick (vv. 17–18). Some of these were seen subsequently (see Acts 16:18; 2:4; 28:3–6; 14:8–10), but they do not seem to be normative.

Jesus, as the triumphant Son of God, then ascended to heaven and was seated at the right hand of God (v. 19), just as He had said earlier (Mark 14:62). Likewise, He will also return in the clouds (13:26–27). This is the glorious gospel, the good news of Jesus Christ, the Son of God (1:1).

Reflect on why the disciples lacked faith and stubbornly refused to believe the three witnesses. What lessons can we learn from this? Mark's gospel is a witness to who Jesus is. Respond to Jesus in worshipful and trusting prayer and thanksgiving.

Jesus sits at the right hand of God (v. 19; Mark 12:36; Acts 2:33; 5:31; Romans 8:34; Ephesians 1:20–23; Hebrews 1:3; 8:1; 1 Peter 3:22). What does this mean to you? What implications are there for global mission and your personal involvement in it?